FOOD AND DRINK

BOOK 5

THE Food & Drink BOOK 5

MICHAEL BARRY
● JILL GOOLDEN ●
CHRIS KELLY

BBC BOOKS

Illustrations: Annie Ellis
Photographs: Sarah Taylor
Stylist: Rosein Neald
Home Economist: Mary Cadogan

Published by BBC Books
A division of BBC Enterprises Limited
Woodlands, 80 Wood Lane
London W12 0TT

First published 1989
© Michael Barry, Jill Goolden, Chris Kelly 1989

ISBN 0 563 20843 0

Colour printing by Lawrence Allen Ltd, Weston-super-Mare
Photosetting by Ace Filmsetting Ltd, Frome, Somerset
Text and cover printed and bound in Great Britain by
Richard Clay Ltd, Bungay, Suffolk

ACKNOWLEDGEMENTS

Food and Drink would like to thank the following for their help in the preparation of this book:

John Anderson
William Banbury
Professor Pierre Budowski
Antonio Carluccio
Oz Clarke
Bernice Clarke
Liz Coleman
Professor Michael Crawford
Wendy Doyle
Vicky Ewart
Geoff Fish
Karen Flower
Richard Guy
Nicky Hughes

Lyn Kennedy
Rosanna Klouda
Stephen McCrum
Susie Magasiner
Gilly Metherell
Gabrielle O'Connor
Tom Seery
Richard Shepherd
The Small Independent
    Brewers' Association
Keith and Jean Turner
Terry Vaughan
David Williams
Harry and Gerry Yeung

CONTENTS

INTRODUCTION

In March 1989, at the end of our most recent series, we celebrated the hundredth edition of *Food and Drink*. It is not necessarily healthy to look back all the time (good television needs new ideas above all else). But I know that Michael Barry, Jill Goolden and Chris Kelly have a justified sense of achievement about this milestone. *Food and Drink* has now broadcast fifty hours of television, and for much of that time (five years, in fact) it has been Britain's top-rated food programme.

Here they have collected the best of the 1988–89 series for your delectation. For those of you who bought one or more of the fact sheets you will find some of those recipes here . . . but much, much more besides. This book contains seventy-five additional recipes from Michael Barry that never appeared in the original series; it has five highly instructive chapters from Jill Goolden about a range of fascinating drinks; and it has a number of highly pertinent pieces by Chris Kelly questioning the state of our food. Chris reviews what has surely been an extraordinary year for those of us who care about our food . . . extraordinary, and at times, alarming.

It was the year in which salmonella finally broke into the public consciousness – and with a vengeance (Chris writes about this in Chapter 4). It was the year of listeria hysteria (the best down-to-earth advice about this is also in Chapter 4). Prolonged public calls were made for a dedicated Ministry of Food to protect the consumers' interests rather than those of the producers. The

Monopolies and Mergers Commission unveiled radical plans for a more competitive brewing industry (Jill looks at whether this really is good news for your local pub in Chapter 10). The list of major stories is legion. Never before has the nation's food supply made front page news week after week (with the possible exception of the Second World War when Britain 'dug for victory').

Regular viewers of *Food and Drink*, however, would have been aware of these stories rather earlier. It was in 1985 that the programme first drew attention to the rapidly rising salmonella poisoning statistics, questioning their cause and examining good food hygiene in the kitchen. It was in 1986 that the programme focused on the inequitable difference between beer prices across the country – something the Monopolies and Mergers Commission now hopes to cure. It was in 1987 that *Food and Drink* first broadcast calls for a dedicated Ministry of Food. That is quite enough backslapping, you may say – and I do not deny there is a little of that involved.

But that is not the point I am really making. For some years *Food and Drink*, along with a few other programmes and magazines, may have banged the drum of food quality. But food was never a front page issue. Even now you can still learn the closing figure of the Dow Jones Index on Wall Street in *News at Ten* every night (of no significance whatsoever to 99 per cent of their viewers). But you would be very lucky if food prices or any other food news is mentioned more than twice a month (of 100 per cent significance to 100 per cent of their viewers). News, I am afraid, needs to satisfy only two criteria: that it is *new*, and that someone (usually a man) sitting in an ivory tower of a newsroom decides it is important.

If you analyse the average contents of a radio or television news bulletin you will find that, quite often, as many as one half of the items are government-inspired. Government policies, debates in the House of Commons and alternative opposition policies are all (quite rightly) news. So the dearth of food news is also a measure of how little importance the political parties attach to the subject. As I write, in April 1989, food once more seems to have taken a back seat, despite all the alarums and excursions of the past six months. Our 1987 call for a new Ministry of Food was made by the distinguished food writer, Geoffrey Cannon. At the time he pointed out that a General Election was imminent and that our viewers should question their candidates closely on food issues and then vote accordingly. The advice, while cleverly conceived, proved to be of little help. *None* of the parties had anything approaching a coherent policy. Perhaps this will now change – and I stress the 'perhaps'. During the recent food crisis various ministers and opposition spokesmen quite clearly did not know what they were talking about and sometimes got things demonstrably wrong. This means that they had not been properly briefed by their advisers and researchers, who in their turn were ill-informed. Public confusion about salmonella and listeria became inevitable when few in Westminster or Whitehall could give clear, unambiguous advice. Will this have been an educative experience for them? Let us hope so.

But we should not be too grim about our food. Not only because eating is as much about enjoyment as it is about sustenance (as Michael's recipes prove), but also because we can take heart from one aspect of the recent dramas I have referred to. For the first time many people are questioning how their food is produced and pondering the way they think it ought to be. Why has salmonella got into eggs? Why do more than half the chickens sold have salmonella in them? Why is listeria found in 'TV dinners'? In this way we begin to learn basic food chemistry and proper food handling – things that post-War generations are woefully ignorant about. But, just as importantly, we begin to demand what sort of food we want – not only in terms of quality and choice but also with reference to the *method* of its production. To this we say, 'Bravo!'. We can take heart, too, because this development is part of a larger process.

During the Second World War (and well into Clement Attlee's siege economy) feeding the nation cheaply on our own resources was a top priority. Farmers and food manufacturers were urged on by the Government, both verbally and economically. These two arms of food production became part of the fabric of government – sitting on ministry committees and helping formulate policy. We now recognise that this resulted in low quality meat with growing bacteriological problems, and tasteless food products stuffed full of additives to give them the appearance of reality. Is this a wild and unsupported generalisation? Read Chapter 4 about poultry and Chapter 9 about bacon and you will begin to see what I mean. And look at the packaging in any supermarket now – see how they positively boast that they have removed additives from food products to get nearer to the real thing.

In the 1950s and 1960s the producers held all the power, in government *and* in the high street. They dictated to retailers what products and produce would be on the shelves. In the 1970s there was a dramatic shift that is now reaching its logical conclusion in the 1980s. The retailers (chiefly, six vast supermarket companies who now sell us at least 60 per cent of our groceries) revolted against low quality, homogenised food. They were much more aware of their customers' feelings than the producers and perceived our dissatisfaction – almost before we realised it ourselves. With their dominance of high streets (and out-of-town shopping centres) they were able to demand better quality. They issued specifications to farmers as to how, for instance, their pigs should be bred. They told manufacturers to remove pointless additives from their products. Admittedly, there is still a long way to go but this shift of power has undoubtedly benefited us. Now I detect it going one step further – we, the consumers, are going to tell the retailers how we would like our meat produced. Yes, we may pay a little more for the privilege. But we want chicken that tastes of chicken (not fish meal – because that is the cheapest feed) and that is not contaminated with salmonella. Some of us want organically grown produce. And do you know what? We are getting it. The real power lies with us because we pay the piper. All we need to do is realise the fact. The retailers did long ago – and the producers are now getting the message too.

Nowhere is the emergence of this new 'consumer-power' more evident than in the field of bio-technology. At the moment we are hovering on the threshold of an entirely new age of agriculture. Mankind has unravelled the mysteries of DNA and begun manufacturing genetic products which can revolutionise food production. Do we *need* this to happen? Do we *want* this to happen? Will we *say* whether we do? Let us look at two current examples – BST in dairy cattle and growth-promoting hormones in beef cattle.

Bovine Somatotropin (BST) is a naturally occurring hormone which can now be manufactured in the test tube. When injected into cows (which already generate the substance themselves) it puts up their milk yield. It is being tested in many countries around the world but has not yet been approved for use. That is the debate – should it be? The arguments against are that we already have a milk surplus in Europe and we do not need any more; that marginal differences between the artificially generated BST and the naturally occurring hormone may have incalculable long-term effects; and that higher milk production per cow may be unkind to the animals. The arguments in favour are that it allows higher milk production from a smaller number of cows; that in parts of the world they have a milk shortage not a surplus; and that it is a naturally occurring hormone aiding a natural process rather than an artificial drug.

On balance you would expect all those concerned with milk production to be in favour of BST because of its economic benefits. But that is by no means the case. It is the drug companies wanting to manufacture BST who are in favour whilst many producers – the Farmers Union of Wales, the Women's Farming Union, the Milk Marketing Board, the International Dairy Federation – oppose it. When you question them you discover that most do not doubt its safety but they fear consumer reaction to it. That, for me, is the most significant part of the whole argument – the producers are giving top priority to our views. To give them our views rationally what we need, of course, is information. Will it surprise you to learn that BST trials were carried out in secret, that the milk entered the milk supply from the unnamed farms and that the results are even now being secretly considered by a government committee? Will it also surprise you to learn that the sort of criteria the committee applies include *safety*, sometimes include *need* and never include whether consumers *want* it? So while the consumers' message seems to have percolated through to many producers it certainly has not been listened to in the machinery of government. It would indeed be bigoted of us to oppose BST merely on the grounds that we do not want our 'daily pinta' – as it were – meddled with, regardless of the arguments. But that is the level of debate we are reduced to if civil servants persist in such absurd secrecy. I would argue that if we do not want BST, *on any grounds*, then we should not have it. But I would certainly prefer our reasons to be logical and well-informed.

The other example is, on the surface, evidence of a consumer victory. In the mid-1980s the EEC banned the use of growth-promoting hormones on beef cattle. It was argued that they were unsafe because the long-term effects on both the animals and the consumers were unknown but possibly dangerous. Various consumer organisations lobbied hard and won – such hormones are now banned in the Common Market. When EEC officials sought to extend the ban to meat imports earlier this year it set off a trade war between the Community and the US. The US Government argued that the hormones they use are entirely safe and that this was merely another way for the EEC to erect trade barriers against them.

There is, in fact, much cause for concern about the hormone ban. In the first place, a commissioned report giving five naturally occurring hormones a clean bill of health was never published; secondly, the ban is ineffectively enforced since several of these hormones are still demonstrably in use; then, where they are not available, other hormones – ones that are well-proven to be highly dangerous – are being used instead; and, finally, the consumer organisations who opposed hormones failed to consult the public very widely before they did so.

It may well be that it is genuinely the view of consumers that they do not want to see growth-promoting hormones used. But it is essential that information on such issues is freely available and widely disseminated. Then we will be able to distinguish the genuine arguments from the ulterior motives. This, perhaps, is the next step in the consumers' long march to achieving control of their food supply.

How, by the same token, can we understand the scope of the current food poisoning epidemic, or comprehend its causes, when government statistics on salmonella outbreaks are kept secret in the restricted 'Communicable Disease Report'? No wonder there is hysteria about listeria – we have been kept in the dark about that too. At least we do now know something about salmonella and listeria. There were serious outbreaks of hepatitis two years ago caused by contaminated shellfish from British coastal waters polluted with sewage. They may have told the doctors and health officers but they never told the public. In truth, there is still a long way to go. That is one important function, we like to think, of *Food and Drink*. To campaign continually for more information, for better educated consumers and for higher quality food.

But it is important to remember that that is not our only function. Self-appointed puritans can get very tedious, can't they? Food, as I said, is as much about enjoyment as anything else. We very much hope that you enjoy making the recipes in this book and following Chris and Jill's practical tips. We look forward to renewing our acquaintance with you on the air in November this year. Until then, *bon appetit!*

Peter Bazalgette
Producer of *Food and Drink*

April 1989

THE 50p CHALLENGE

MEALS ON A BUDGET
MICHAEL BARRY

The idea for these recipes came from watching restaurateur and writer Antonio Carluccio cooking lunch for a London fire station on a small fixed budget – one of our recent *Food and Drink* challenges. I wondered just how small a fixed budget could be without becoming impossible. It's not such an easy question to answer – you have to take a couple of things into consideration. For instance, can you do a bulk buy, or do you have to buy things individually each time? It's much cheaper in bulk, and you can provide much more variety in depth – a chicken, far too expensive for only one meal for two, can provide the basis for at least four dishes spread over a week. Grilled garlic breasts could be one, a casserole could be made with the legs, the wings and carcass trimmings used to fill pancakes or pasties, and the bones for soup. The other key question is what about extras – salt and pepper, oil, herbs, sugar, cornflour and the other store-cupboard basics? It would be impossible to do super low budget meals without some of these to hand. But buying them in anything less than bulk is impossible and it makes the exercise likewise!

I'm going to suggest four meals for two people at 50 pence per head. A pound per meal for two that is – each with two courses. And as far as the two key questions are concerned I've decided to make it difficult in one instance and easy in the other. The difficult bit is that I'm not bulk buying. The main ingredients for each meal will be bought on separate shopping trips. It provides freshness and the more frequent shopping protects the nutritional value of the ingredients. I am, though, going to assume that I've already got herbs and condiments, sugar and oil etc. But to be scrupulously fair I am going to charge a basic 5p per meal for these 'extras'. (All prices are right at the time of writing.) So – here goes . . .

· MEAL 1

CHICKEN LIVER AND PEAS PILAU

SYRIAN ORANGES

Serves 2

This is a meal with a Middle Eastern flavour. The pilau is light and colourful as well as extremely nutritious. The flavours and combinations are common right from Turkey down to the Egyptian border. The pudding is sweet and tart at the same time, an easy crafty way of using a fruit that we far too often take for granted. It makes a splendid contrast to the rich but quite dry main course.

Unless you have an amazing butcher, your best bet for chicken livers is the freezer compartment of your supermarket. They come in 8 oz (225 g) tubs and are extraordinarily good value. Don't be tempted to buy pre-prepared packet rice. It is very expensive and lacks the flavour of good long-grain rice. The flavourings are exotic sounding but very common in the eastern Mediterranean. They used to be common in Britain too, strangely enough, but fell out of use in the eighteenth century and have only made a comeback with our taste for Indian food. For the pudding buy naval oranges if you can or jaffas (they hold together better when sliced).

Chicken Liver Peas and Pilau

1 oz (25 g) butter
½ onion, chopped   5p
8 oz (225 g) long-grain rice   11p
Salt and pepper
¾ pint (450 ml) water
4 oz (100 g) frozen peas   10p
8 oz (225 g) chicken livers   40p
½ teaspoon ground coriander
½ teaspoon ground cinnamon
1 tablespoon oil

Syrian Oranges
2 firm oranges   25p
2 oz (50 g) sugar
4 fl oz (120 ml) water
2 cloves
Extras   5p

TOTAL 96p

Chicken Liver Peas and Pilau
Melt the butter in a large frying pan and gently fry the onion for 2 minutes. Add the rice, season with salt and pepper and turn for 1 minute. Add the water, bring to the boil, cover and simmer for 15 minutes. Stir in the peas. Cover and set aside with a cloth over the rice and under the lid. Rinse the livers and fry them with the spices in the oil for 3 minutes until well browned but not dry. Season. Arrange the rice in a ring on a serving plate, put the livers in the centre and serve.

Syrian Oranges
Cut the rind off one orange, remove the pith and slice the rind into matchsticks. You can buy a gadget to do this. Put the matchsticks in a pan of cold water, bring them to the boil and then drain. Return them to the pan with the sugar, water and cloves, bring to the boil and simmer for 10 minutes. Cool. Peel the other orange and cut both oranges into ¼-in (5-mm) slices. Pour the syrup and peel over the oranges and chill for 1 hour before serving.

MEAL 2

SAUSAGE AND BEAN CASSEROLE

BAKED SPICED APPLES
Serves 2
The main course of this meal is adapted from one of the national dishes of France – Cassoulet. Essentially it's a bean bake – a dish of dried beans soaked, cooked till almost tender and then flavoured and enriched. As you would expect with the French, when they enrich, they enrich! Preserved goose, pieces of roast lamb, special sausages and so on. But a very acceptable – indeed delicious – version can be made simply. When you buy the beans don't buy the big type of butter beans. Good haricot beans are round and kidney-shaped and often quite small – when they are dry. They expand remarkably when they are soaked. It is tradi-

tional to use white beans for this, but kidney beans do come in all colours: red, green, black and spotted. There's no reason not to choose another colour if you fancy it. (If you are using dried red kidney beans remember to boil them thoroughly for at least 15 minutes.) As for the sausages, I prefer beef or the lamb sausages that seem to be creeping onto the market. Sausages with some texture are certainly nicer. *Don't* use frankfurters. For the baked apple there are two choices. Bramleys or other traditional cookers are fine but tend to bake to a pulp. I prefer a good eating apple – more flavour and more bite – it's a matter of personal taste as the prices aren't that different.

Sausage and Bean Casserole
8 oz (225 g) beans   15p
8 oz (225 g) beef chipolatas   35p
1 onion, thinly sliced   10p
1 clove garlic, chopped
2 tablespoons oil
1 tablespoon tomato purée   5p
Salt and pepper
Seasonings
4 oz (100 g) breadcrumbs   5p

Baked Spiced Apples
2 good English apples   20p
2 tablespoons brown sugar
½ teaspoon ground cloves
½ teaspoon ground cinnamon
1 cup water
Extras   5p

TOTAL 95p

Sausage and Bean Casserole
Soak the beans in a large saucepan of fresh water for at least 4 to 6 hours. Change the water, and cover the beans by at least 2 in (5 cm). Bring to the boil, boil for 10 minutes, then simmer for 1½ hours (a low 300°F (150°C), gas mark 2). Pre-heat the oven to 350°F (180°C), gas mark 4. Fry the sausages, onion and garlic in the oil until brown. Stir the tomato purée into the cooked beans, which should have absorbed the water but be moist. Add the sausage mixture, stirring gently. Season generously, adding herbs to taste – thyme and marjoram are nice. Cover with the breadcrumbs and bake for 30 minutes (to an hour). Serve in soup plates.

Baked Spiced Apples
Core the apples and cut a shallow line around the equator with a sharp knife. Mix the sugar and spices. Place the apples in an ovenproof dish. Fill the core holes with the sugar, pour the water over and bake for 40 minutes, the same temperature as the beans, in the same oven. When serving, pour the juices over the apples.

MEAL 3

PARSLEY, PARSNIP AND CHEESE SOUP

TORTILLA AND SPINACH SALAD

Serves 2

There's an Iberian flavour to this meal. I find patterns of balanced eating usually have a common national or regional flavour and style, probably the result of countless generations of experiment and experience in producing balanced meals from basic local ingredients. I must admit the Parsley, Parsnip and Cheese Soup isn't very Spanish, but the parsnip replaces the sweet potatoes or yams, which were common currency in Spain's erstwhile South American empire, with the same combinations of solidity and sweetness. The tortilla, on the other hand, is strictly traditional. It's quite delicious enough to cook in its own right, but it's also great for using up left-overs or small quantities of delicious things there are not enough of to go around on their own – mushrooms, prawns, peppers, cooked meat. All are fine on a less restricted budget. The trick with the omelette is to cook it *thick*! Use a pan small enough for the mixture to be an inch (2.5 cm) thick. In the unlikely event of you having any left over, it is delicious cut into squares or wedges and eaten cold. In fact, in Spain it is a traditional hors d'oeuvre or *tapas* – a snack to have with a pre-dinner drink. For the salad, trust me, raw spinach is delicious like this and very refreshing.

Parsley, Parsnip and Cheese Soup
8 oz (225 g) parsnip   10p
½ onion   5p
1 tablespoon oil
Salt and pepper
1 pint (600 ml) water
1½ oz (40 g) Cheddar cheese, grated   10p
1 tablespoon chopped parsley

Tortilla

8 oz (225 g) onions   10p
1 lb (450 g) potatoes   15p
3 tablespoons oil   5p
Salt and pepper
4 eggs   30p
½ teaspoon basil (optional)
½ teaspoon thyme (optional)

Spinach Salad

4 oz (100 g) spinach leaves, cleaned   10p
Salt and pepper
1 tablespoon honey
1 tablespoon lemon juice
2 tablespoons oil
Extras   5p

TOTAL £1.00

Parsley, Parsnip and Cheese Soup
Peel the parsnip and onion and cut them into small pieces. Heat the oil in a large frying pan, add the parsnip and onion and fry gently for 2 minutes. Season and add the water. Simmer for 20 minutes, then liquidise or blend until smooth. Return the mixture to the pan. Add the grated cheese, heating gently until melted. Stir in the chopped parsley, adjust the seasoning to taste and serve hot.

Tortilla
Peel the onions, scrub the potatoes and cut both into ½-inch (1-cm) dice. Boil the potatoes in salted water for 5 minutes while frying the onion gently in the oil in a maximum 7-in (18-cm) frying pan. Drain the potato and add to the frying pan. Fry for 5 minutes more, season well. Beat the eggs and add the basil and thyme, if you wish. Pour over the potatoes and cook, stirring gently, until set. Place under a heated grill until the top browns and bubbles. Cut into wedges and serve with the salad.

Spinach Salad
Wash the spinach leaves and tear them into 50 pence-sized pieces. Season. Heat the honey and lemon juice gently together in a saucepan until the honey melts. Add the oil and heat gently. When hot, pour over the spinach.

MEAL 4

LEMON SARDINES

COURGETTE AND NUT PASTA

Serves 2

This is a meal to delight the eye as well as please the palate and ease the purse. The colours are as bright as the Italian sunshine that inspires the flavours. If you were feeling flush, and willing to splash out another 20p on the meal, you could substitute broccoli for the courgettes. A slightly more sophisticated taste, but no more delicious or nutritious. When you are shopping for the meal look at the sardine tins carefully. The prices vary greatly and often for no real reason as far as the contents are concerned. Portuguese sardines are usually best at the cheaper end of the market, but you can find a bargain. Don't buy fish in tomato sauce; they really will not go well with this recipe. As to the main course, you can use wholemeal, white or egg pasta, as you choose. The shape that seems best suited to this kind of cooking is the spiral or corkscrew shape. They have more bulk and mix better with the vegetables than long thin spaghetti or flat noodles. The method for preparing the pasta, by the way, is a crafty speciality, great for fuel economy as well as being foolproof – or at least proof against the kind of concentration lapse that with conventional methods can turn pasta to congealed wallpaper paste in five minutes of overcooking.

Lemon Sardines
2 lemons   15p
1 × 4½-oz (120-g) tin of sardines in oil   45p
Salt and pepper

Courgette and Nut Pasta
6 oz (175 g) spiral pasta   12p
2 pints (1.2 litres) water
8 oz (225 g) courgettes   12p
1 cup milk   6p
1 tablespoon cornflour
1 tablespoon butter
1 tablespoon grated Parmesan cheese
1 oz (25 g) salted peanuts   5p
Salt and pepper
Extras   5p

TOTAL £1.00

Lemon Sardines

Cut the top off each lemon like a lid and trim the bottoms so they stand upright. Hold the lemon over a bowl, and scoop out the insides with a sharp spoon. Open the sardines and mash them with the oil, seasoning and about one-third of the lemon pulp and juice. (Check for your own taste as you do this.) Fill the lemon shells with the sardine mixture and place on individual plates. Place the lids at a jaunty angle and chill for ½ an hour before serving.

Courgette and Nut Pasta

Pre-heat the oven to 350°F (180°C), gas mark 4. Put the pasta in a saucepan with 2 pints (1.2 litres) of boiling salted water. Boil for 3 minutes. Now for the crafty bit. Turn off the heat, cover and leave to stand for about 7 minutes. Drain. Meanwhile trim the courgettes, slice into 1-in (2.5-cm) lengths and cut these into quarters lengthwise. Make a white sauce by whisking the milk, cornflour and butter together. Bring to the boil, whisking twice as you go. Mix the pasta, courgettes, and white sauce together. Season generously and pour into a baking or gratin dish. Sprinkle with the cheese and peanuts and bake in the oven for 30 minutes until browned and bubbling.

PACKED LUNCHES AND PICNICS

INTRODUCTION
CHRIS KELLY

According to Tom Seery, Catering Services Manager for the borough of Hillingdon: 'the school meals service generally regards packed lunches as public enemy number one'. At least that used to be the case. Now, largely thanks to the energy and marketing skills of people like Tom himself, the school lunch box is being transformed. Before we see how, consider for a moment the long, slow decline of the school meals service since the Second World War.

Recognising that the special problems of war-time made school meals a necessity for school children, the Government required local authorities to provide them and contributed 95 per cent of the money. By 1947, the State was paying the full cost. In 1965, nutritional guidelines were introduced recommending that school meals should provide one-third of a child's daily calorie, protein and vitamin needs. The price of the meal was set nationally, though children from needy families would still be fed free of charge.

1980, however, marked a watershed in the service. Under the new Education Act, local authorities were no longer obliged to offer meals for all children who wanted them, though the rights of children from hard-up families were still protected. Meanwhile the nutritional guidelines were abandoned, as was price control. The Government was looking to save £190m in grants.

Ironically, the same fateful year saw the publication of a DHSS report called 'Inequalities in Health'. Its findings were unequivocal:

'It should be regarded as a matter of importance – on education and health grounds – to ensure that all children receive a school meal or an adequate substitute . . . To leave schoolchildren . . . to make their own free choices as to what food is to be purchased would be wrong. Children will frequently prefer to consume foods high only in sugar and other sources of energy.'

The report went on to recommend that local authorities should be required to provide nutritionally adequate meals at all schools, free of charge. The proposals never stood a chance, however, since even in the foreword the Secretary of State for Social Services, Patrick Jenkin, said the extra money involved – some £2 billion a year – 'is quite unrealistic in present or any foreseeable economic circumstances . . .' Observers might have been forgiven for wondering how 'realistic' it was to put at potential risk the future of millions of our children.

Following the Social Security Act of 1986, the right to free school meals was removed from an estimated 50 000 more children who until then had qualified for them on the grounds of hardship. And this at a time when 80 per cent of mothers interviewed for a Child Poverty Action Group survey said the free school meal their child had been getting was his/her main meal of the day.

Largely as a result of these cutbacks, between the years 1979 and 1987, the proportion of children eating school dinners nationwide declined dramatically – from around 65 per cent to 37 per cent. Another contributory factor to the fall-off has been defined by Tom Seery as 'the sandwich culture', particularly prevalent among primary school children. Regiments of them would turn up with gaily coloured plastic boxes decorated with Snoopies and other favourite heroes from comics and television. Inside was further confirmation that the children understood the message, if not yet the power, of the medium. Crisps, chocolate bars and biscuits were the order of the day, washed down with cola or other sugary drinks; bearing out the gloomy prophecy of the report we saw earlier, 'Inequalities in Health'. Naturally manufacturers were quick to identify and exploit a vast, and growing, market.

Besides the drop in demand for school meals, and the increasing substitution of junk foods, concerned officers in local authority catering departments had to face a third challenge. The Government has decreed that their services be put out to compulsory competitive tender. This means that if private firms prove they can do the job better and more cheaply, they'll win the contract. The introduction of an element of rivalry, which may or may not prove to be a good thing, has at least helped to galvanise the more caring and innovative authorities into action.

At a conference in the autumn of 1987, the National Association of School Meals Organisers met the crisis head on. Among the crucial lessons they learned was the importance of marketing techniques. Though they had begun to improve standards considerably in response to reports like NACNE and COMA, they were failing to get the message across to their young customers.

The meeting gave birth to FEAST – Fun Eating At School Today – which was officially launched in January 1989. The campaign has a number of aims: to promote healthy eating, thus increasing meal numbers and becoming more cost-effective for competitive tendering; to improve the image of school catering nationally, and to encourage greater co-operation between authorities. So far some 70 per cent of local authorities representing 20 000 schools have taken part in the project, and it's clearly an enormous success.

Nowhere is FEAST more vigorous than in the London borough of Hillingdon. Tom Seery, the passionately committed thirty-seven year-old ex-restaurateur in charge of schools' catering there, took me to three schools where the scheme is in varying stages of development. At the Douay Martyrs School in Ickenham we had lunch with enthusiastic pupils and staff, who've been entirely won over by the transformation. Gone is the old image of stodge and overcooked cabbage, followed by jam tart and watery custard. This was a restaurant, not a canteen, with lively pop music on the loudspeakers, colourful art-work on the walls and an appetising choice of healthy, beautifully presented food, both hot and cold – made entirely from fresh ingredients. Characteristic of Tom's approach is the ice-cream. He knows children love it, so instead of banning it, or forcing his young customers out of the gates for it, he has installed ice-cream machines which produce a low-fat, home-made variety – perfectly acceptable as part of a balanced diet. As a result of this consumer-led philosophy, an astonishing 92 per cent of the Douay Martyrs children eat the school lunch. It's simply too good to miss.

At the nearby Hayes Manor School they were still in the planning phase, looking forward to a spring opening of the Pillars restaurant. Classes throughout the school had been consulted on what they wanted to see. Top of their priorities was 'no queueing', so a novel system of gold, silver and bronze vouchers has been devised, eliminating the need to pay on the spot and so speeding the flow. The menu is varied and exciting; they even hope to have summer barbecues. The quadrophonic speakers are already in place; posters are being designed in the art department, and the scheme is generating excitement in staff and pupils alike. Excitement about school food! A revolution indeed.

And that brings us full circle, back to the lunch box. At the Charville Infant and Junior School not only do the meals offer quite superb quality and choice (infants 64p, juniors 74p) but also a brilliant new idea has been introduced by Tom Seery: the designer lunch box. Children who prefer a cold, picnic-type meal leave their plastic boxes at school and choose what goes into them from an appealing, healthy, balanced list of possibles, including drinks like pure apple and orange juice. Phyllis Casselton, the cook-in-charge, and her dedicated staff – all specially trained for the FEAST scheme like their colleagues in other FEAST schools – fill the boxes each day and wash them when the children go home. Small wonder that since the project was introduced, 100 per cent of the infants have opted for eating food provided at the school, whether hot or cold, and take-up among the juniors has risen by 40 per cent. By contrast I sneaked a look at one of the comparatively few lunch boxes still brought from home. It contained an already-opened bag of crisps and an empty Thermos flask. Its young owner had every right to feel deprived.

Thanks to generous support from industry, and the fact that increased demand has helped make it self-financing, the FEAST campaign has cost the ratepayer nothing. FEAST 2 is due in the spring of 1990. By making today's children aware of the importance and appeal of healthy eating, using the marketing techniques they understand, the movement is helping create the more discerning adult of tomorrow. In consequence it's not too much to hope that British catering standards in general will rise. This can only happen, however, if all local authorities see the eminent sense of the scheme, and competitive tendering does not promote profit-making at the expense of our children's well-being.

RECIPES
MICHAEL BARRY

With few things are the differences in taste between children and adults more clear than with packed lunches or picnics. It may be unfair to say that two packets of crisps and two chocolate bars would suit most kids – but not too unfair. Adults, on the other hand, can soon tire of even the most delicious sandwiches. I can remember a time as a young lad working on a building site when plain, dry bread would have seemed preferable to the third consecutive week of pilchard-in-tomato-sauce-sarnies. Ah – ungrateful youth!

I've gathered here, then, some ideas, suggestions and combinations that should spice up or rejuvenate the palate of the young and not-so-young eating away from home; though most do make nice nosh at the kitchen table too. At the sophisticated end of the sandwich family comes the Scandinavian open sandwich – more for Glyndebourne and Henley than a classroom snack for the lower fifth. The crucial thing about them is secure and reasonably flat transportation. A definite case of 'hampers anyone?' Anyway – whether you make 'open' or 'closed' sandwiches here are three delicious toppings or fillings.

SMOKED SALMON CORNETS

Serves 1

Grand, delicious, extremely attractive and not as crucially expensive as they seem. Cream cheese isn't that costly, you see.

2 postcard-sized slices smoked salmon
4 oz (100 g) low fat cream cheese
1 lemon

Simply spread the cream cheese over a piece of smoked salmon then roll it up to form a cone shape. You may find it easier to roll the salmon up first, then pipe in the cream cheese filling. This should be placed on well buttered bread. Use a French stick which has been sliced horizontally. To decorate, use thinly sliced lemon cut in half, place these along the smoked salmon cone; you can squeeze them on to it when you eat it.

CHICKEN AND WALNUTS

Serves 1

While this is delicious piled high for grown ups, you can leave out the walnuts and put another slice of bread on top for the school lunch box with great success.

Lettuce
6 oz (175 g) cooked chicken off the bone
2 oz (50 g) walnut pieces
2 tablespoons mayonnaise

Shred the lettuce into fine strips. Mix the rest of the ingredients together. Put the lettuce on to well buttered bread (use wholemeal ideally), pile on the chicken mix and finally decorate with a few twists of lettuce and a couple of walnuts.

COURGETTE BUTTER

Serves 1

Courgette Butter is really a vegetarian pâté. As well as using it on open sandwiches, it makes a good starter served in individual pots with good crisp toast.

2 oz (50 g) butter
4 courgettes, sliced
½ large or 1 small onion, sliced
Salt and pepper
1 hard-boiled egg, sliced

Melt half the butter and gently sauté the vegetables until they are very soft, season with salt and pepper and add the other half of the butter. Tip into a food processor and blend until smooth. Turn into small ramekins or bowls and chill for 15 minutes. Spread on to buttered bread, I use a cottage loaf, and decorate with slices of hard-boiled egg.

RELISHES

When bread dominates the meal a good relish or chutney to add a spice to the appetite makes all the difference. Here are three with some ideas for using them.

It is best to use stainless steel or ceramic pans for boiling vinegar rather than aluminium or copper which react against the acidity (see box). The glass jars used in all preserving must be sterilised thoroughly, either by boiling or soaking in a disinfectant solution suitable for use on babies' bottles. It is also important to use jars with non-corrosive lids, preferably with rubber seals.

PICKLED ONIONS

Makes 2 × 1¾-pint (1-l) jars

This is my grandmother's recipe for pickled onions, with a touch of sweetness to balance the bite. As the pickle part of a ploughman's lunch they are perfect. Try sticks of three cheeses (Cheddar, Wensleydale and Stilton for choice) with a couple of crusty rolls to complete the meal.

The quantities of onions and vinegar used in this recipe vary according to the size of your jars.

1 lb (450 g) pickling onions
2 oz (50 g) sea salt
1 pint (600 ml) light or dark malt vinegar
3 oz (75 g) light soft brown sugar
2 tablespoons pickling spice
Muslin and a little string to tie up the pickling spices
2 × 1¾-pint (1-l) glass jars

To peel the onions drop them into boiling water for 1 minute, then run them under cold water to stop the cooking. Remove the skins, and put the onions in a shallow dish, sprinkle with salt and leave for 6 hours. Rinse and wait till they dry before proceeding. Boil the vinegar and sugar together until the sugar dissolves, add the bag of spices and simmer for 5 minutes. Put the onions in the jars and pour the hot vinegar over them. Close the lid and leave for 2 weeks before eating.

PICKLED CUCUMBERS
Makes 1 × 1¾-pint (1-l) jar

In America they call these bread and butter pickles because they make a good sandwich filling on their own. I like to add a little cottage cheese or cheese spread, but the Americans aren't that wrong!

Pickling cucumbers are ideal, but ordinary cucumbers will do just as well.

4 pickling cucumbers or 1 large ordinary cucumber
1 oz (25 g) sea salt
1 pint (600 ml) cider vinegar
1 pint (600 ml) water that has been boiled
4-6 oz (100–175 g) preserving sugar (depending on how sweet you like your pickles)
1 teaspoon dried dill seeds
Sprig of fresh dill if available

Use a Mandolin or processor to slice the cucumbers into ½-in (1-cm) slices. You can buy a Mandolin at catering equipment shops and kitchen departments of major department stores. Salt the cucumbers and leave for 1 hour, rinse and pack tightly into a 1¾-pint (1-l) jar. Boil the vinegar, water, sugar and dill seeds together until a light syrup forms. Pour over the cucumbers while hot, add the fresh dill and seal. These will be ready to eat in a few days.

MANGO AND GRAPE CHUTNEY
Makes about 3 lb (1.5 kg)

A rich luxurious chutney good enough to give away as presents in small jars at Christmas. If you plan to eat it yourself, try it on thick slices of tongue and turkey sandwiched together with the pickle before being put between the buttered halves of long crisp rolls. Wow! (The Wow! is partly the flavour and partly the heat. If you don't like hot foods you can cut down on the mustard seed and chillies.)

1 pint (600 ml) cider vinegar
2 oz (50 g) sugar
1 lb 2 oz (500 g) green grapes
2 oz (50 g) currants
2 oz (50 g) sultanas
2 oz (50 g) raisins
2 oz (50 g) whole mustard seed
5 oz (150 g) candied peel
5 oz (150 g) stem ginger
1 oz (25 g) sea salt
2 cloves garlic (optional)
4 dried red chillies, chopped
1 lb (450 g) tinned mango

Boil the vinegar and sugar together. Add the other ingredients except the mango and cook for 25 minutes, until the liquid has thickened. Drain and chop the mango and add, cooking for a further 5 minutes. Pour into jars and seal. The chutney will be at its best 2 weeks after making, as all the flavours will have had a chance to mingle.

Aluminium and copper

Acidic foods (of which chutney is an example with its use of vinegar) can attack metal containers and saucepans so that minute quantities of the metal can enter the food. In fact such 'migration' is common with most food containers. It only causes concern when:

1 The migration is more intense than usual.

2 The substance migrating could cause us harm when ingested.

So you should not make chutney in *copper* pans because the vinegar will react with the copper to form poisonous copper salts.

The advice about *aluminium* saucepans is less clear cut. Doctors have evidence that suggests long-term ingestion of aluminium can lead to premature senility (Alzheimer's Disease) in later life. Acidic foods such as tomatoes, rhubarb and jam will greatly increase the amount of aluminium which leaches out of a saucepan into food. Tomato-topped pizza stored in aluminium foil for any length of time will dissolve the foil and form small holes. There is no hard evidence that this will harm us – merely cause for concern that it might if done regularly. Here are some common sense tips.

1 Avoid regular use of aluminium saucepans and foil with acidic foods.

2 Non-stick aluminium saucepans greatly reduce any migration that might take place.

3 Replace saucepans where the non-stick surface has worn away.

PIZZAS

I include here some pizza recipes. Although I prefer my pizzas hot out of the oven, a lot of workplaces and some schools now offer microwave facilities to heat up food and if that's your good fortune pizzas are an ideal candidate. I've given here my crafty pizza base for real, almost instant, start-from-scratch pizzas. But at a pinch most of these toppings work well on split French bread that isn't too crisp to start with.

The quantities for the toppings below are for one pizza. All the pizzas should be cooked on a pre-heated baking tray in a hot oven 425°F (220°C), gas mark 7 for 15 minutes.

PIZZA DOUGH

Makes 3 to 4 pizza bases

Traditional pizza comes from Naples where it is cooked in a bee-hive oven with a beech wood fire. You may not have one in your kitchen but you can still get quite close to the original recipe.

1 oz (25 g) fresh yeast
½ teaspoon sugar
½ pint (300 ml) warm water
¼ teaspoon ascorbic acid (vitamin C, from chemists)
1 lb (450 g) bread flour
¼ teaspoon salt
6 tablespoons olive oil

Dissolve the yeast and sugar in the warm water. Leave to stand until the yeast begins to ferment and froths, approximately 7 minutes. Add the ascorbic acid. Put the flour and salt into a bowl and add the yeast/water and olive oil. Knead into a sticky dough; you may need to add more flour if it is impossibly sticky. Place the dough in a clean oiled bowl, cover with cling film and leave to rise for 15 minutes in a warm place. Divide into 3 or 4 depending on the size of pizza you want. With floured hands work the dough into balls and then flatten and stretch into flat rounds on a heavily floured board. Crimp the edges into a shallow ridge to neaten the shape and help stop the topping from running off the sides. The dough can also be made in a food processor.

MARINARA
Makes 1 pizza

1 tablespoon tomato purée
4 tablespoons fresh or drained tinned tomatoes, chopped
4 tablespoons tinned tuna fish
8 tinned anchovy fillets
8 stoned black olives
Olive oil

Spread the tomato purée on to the dough with the back of a spoon. Mix the tomato and tuna together in a small bowl and spread on top of the purée. Decorate with the anchovies and olives and finally pour on a little olive oil. Bake as above.

MARGHERITA
Makes 1 pizza

1 tablespoon tomato purée
4 tablespoons fresh or drained tinned tomatoes, chopped
4 tablespoons grated Mozzarella cheese
1 teaspoon dried basil
1 teaspoon dried oregano
Olive oil

Spread the tomato purée on to the pizza dough with the back of a spoon. Then spread on the fresh tomato, sprinkle on the Mozzarella, herbs and swizzle on some olive oil. Bake as above.

MUSHROOM
Makes 1 pizza

Olive oil
1 clove garlic, crushed (optional)
4 tablespoons grated Mozzarella cheese
4 oz (100 g) mushrooms, sliced
1 tablespoon freshly grated Parmesan cheese

Drizzle a little oil on to the pizza dough and add the garlic, if using. Sprinkle on the Mozzarella, then the mushrooms and Parmesan. Drizzle a little more olive oil on top and bake as above.

DOUBLE MOZZARELLA
Makes 1 pizza

8 tablespoons grated Mozzarella cheese
4 tablespoons olive oil
1 clove garlic, chopped
2 tablespoons grated Parmesan cheese
Salt and pepper

Spread half the Mozzarella on the base, then sprinkle with the oil and garlic. Add the rest of the Mozzarella, then the Parmesan. Season and bake as above.

SALAMI
Makes 1 pizza

4 tablespoons tomato purée
1 teaspoon basil
1 teaspoon oregano
2 tablespoons grated Parmesan cheese
8 slices salami (or 12 oz (350 g) pepperoni)
Black pepper

Spread the tomato purée on the pizza base with the back of a spoon. Sprinkle on the herbs and cheese and top with an overlapping ring of sliced salami or pepperoni. Grind over some black pepper and bake as above.

COURGETTE AND PEPPER
Makes 1 pizza

14 oz (400 g) courgettes
½ red pepper
½ green pepper
Salt
4 tablespoons tomato purée
½ teaspoon garlic salt
2 tablespoons olive oil

Trim and slice the courgettes and peppers very thinly. Sprinkle the courgettes with salt and leave them to drain for 10 minutes; rinse and dry. Spread the tomato purée over the base, sprinkle with the garlic salt and lay the pepper and courgette slices in attractive patterns. Drizzle the oil over and bake as above.

SOUPS

Here are two soups that travel well. A wide mouthed flask is the best way to transport soups for picnics or packed lunches.

CRAFTY CHICKEN NOODLE SOUP
Serves 1

4 oz (100 g) Vermicelli or fine rice noodles
1½ pints (900 ml) chicken stock (preferably home-made by simmering a chicken carcass with an onion, carrot and bay leaf for between 45 minutes and 1 hour, then straining)
4 spring onions
½ red pepper, diced
1 tablespoon soy sauce

Boil the noodles in the seasoned stock for 3 minutes. Trim and chop the spring onions, green and all, and add to the soup with the diced pepper. Mix in the soy sauce and put immediately, without further cooking, in the flask. The noodles will finish cooking with the vegetables in the flask.

TOMATO AND ORANGE SOUP
Serves 1

This may seem an extremely crafty soup, and it is. But it's also remarkably appealing to young and old, and can be dressed up with slices of decorated oranges and herbs for the smartest dinner party. Don't be tempted to substitute for the ingredients – it tastes best like this – really.

1 onion, finely chopped
2 tablespoons olive or ground nut oil
18 fl oz (500 ml) passatta (thick sieved tomato)
1 cup high juice orange squash
Salt and pepper
1 cup water

Fry the onion gently in the oil for 5 minutes. Add the tomato juice and squash, season with salt and pepper and simmer for 20 minutes. If it gets too thick add the cup of water. Check the seasoning, then pour the hot soup into the flask.

TRAVELLING SALADS

Both of these delicious salads are robust enough to be dressed hours before eating and so they travel really well. I've suggested a dressing that will suit either, but if you have your favourite – do try it instead. A secure plastic snap-top box makes transportation and serving easy and neat.

CHICORY AND ORANGE SALAD

Serves 1

Crisp and tangy, you can make this with either the little bullet-shaped chicory or the bigger leafed 'sugar loaf' kind that is now sometimes available.

2 heads chicory
1 orange
Vinaigrette dressing (below)

Slice the chicory into ½-in (1-cm) rounds, peel the orange and cut into slices of the same thickness. Toss in the dressing and serve.

CHINESE LEAF AND RED PEPPER SALAD

Serves 1

This is one of the prettiest of salads with a good crunchy bite to it, so it's filling as well.

½ Chinese leaf
1 large red pepper
Vinaigrette dressing (below)

Slice the Chinese leaf into ½-in (1-cm) rounds. Finely slice the red pepper. Toss in the salad dressing.

VINAIGRETTE DRESSING

2 tablespoons cider or wine vinegar
2 tablespoons lemon juice
1 teaspoon caster sugar
½ teaspoon salt
8 tablespoons salad oil (half olive, half sunflower, ideally)

Mix the vinegar, lemon juice, sugar and salt until dissolved. Add the oil and mix until thick.

CHICKEN DIPPERS

Serves 1

You can make Dippers yourself by dipping ½-in (1-cm) sticks of chicken breast into beaten egg and then breadcrumbs, and then deep frying them. Although I'm not a great fan of many 'convenience' foods, for a child's lunch box, I think many of the chicken 'goujon' style products on sale chilled or frozen are a good, quick alternative to the deep fryer. This is not least because they can be oven baked, cutting down on fats and smells. Either way, here is a tasty dip for them when they are cold (or hot as an hors d'oeuvre or fancy party treat).

5 oz (150 g) carton of plain yoghurt
2-in (5-cm) slice cucumber, grated
2 tablespoons mango chutney, chopped fine if necessary
½ teaspoon mild curry powder
½ teaspoon salt

Mix all the ingredients together thoroughly. Leave for 20 minutes and use as a dip for the chicken.

DECAFFEINATED DEBRIEF

DECAFFEINATED TEA AND COFFEE

JILL GOOLDEN

It can seem as though everything – everything enjoyable, that is – does you harm these days. You're not even safe with your good old cuppa anymore, it would appear. Caffeine (present, of course, in tea as well as coffee), has been blamed for all manner of malaises. I have on my desk a paper implicating this natural stimulant ('probably the world's most popular drug', according to the British Medical Journal) with almost every type of physical problem: breast lumpiness, strain on the kidneys, promoting high cholesterol levels, increasing the risk of coronary heart disease, causing anxiety neurosis, reducing the body's iron absorption, migraine, foetal damage . . . The list is appalling, and certainly seems to provide a strong enough case for us all to add coffee, tea, cola drinks, chocolate (what ever else?) to the list of things we must definitely try to *give up*.

But before you throw all your jars, packets and cans straight into the dustbin (or yourself off the nearest bridge), wait to hear the good news (you certainly deserve it). Dr Margaret Ashwell, Scientific Director of the British Nutrition Foundation, says she has been unable to find sufficient medical evidence to prove any of these serious allegations. And Dr David Pearson, an allergy specialist at the Withington Hospital in Manchester, adds that 'it is very popular at the moment to think you are allergic to things, especially coffee, and this often isn't the case'. In an article on 'Caffeine and Health', the British Medical Journal states that 'caffeine, except perhaps at very high levels of intake, appears blameless as a risk to bodily health'. Phew!

'Attention,' the article goes on to say 'now centres on caffeine's psychotropic [that is behavioural] effects and addictive properties and its effects on psychological health.' There is no doubt at all that caffeine is a stimulant to the central nervous system affecting each individual in different ways, with various groups of people being more susceptible than others.

But what precisely are the behavioural and psychological effects? Are our lives really affected by the odd cup of coffee or tea? As a stimulant to the nervous system, a cup or two of coffee wakes you up and aids concentration, helping you to feel more alert and less tired (sounds good to me). But if you are particularly sensitive to caffeine, the downside of this is that you may then have difficulty going to sleep, particularly as you get older (sensitivity to caffeine seems to increase with age). Your sleep time may be reduced and the quality of your sleep may even be lowered. As far as behavioural effects are concerned, caffeine may change your mood, at best raising your spirits, at worst promoting transitory (and dose related) anxiety, nervousness and irritability.

Pregnant women may retain caffeine for up to three times as long as is usual in adults, whereas smokers eliminate caffeine twice as quickly as non-smokers. This may well explain why pregnant women often develop an aversion to coffee and why heavy smokers are frequently heavy coffee drinkers as well.

The addictive properties of coffee are certainly all too clear to me. Deciding to purge the system, I cut out coffee (along with all the other 'suspect' pleasures) altogether and felt none the better at all for my supposedly improved diet. The most obvious unpleasant effect was a black cloud of a headache, filling the skull with a dull thud. As the days wore on, so the headache got worse. 'Have a cup of coffee,' a friend suggested. I had never heard of coffee as a headache cure before, but decided nevertheless to give it a try (I'd have tried anything within reason), but magically the coffee worked.

I discovered I was suffering from Caffeine Withdrawal Syndrome, meaning that my body had become used to caffeine and its effects and wasn't too happy when it was withdrawn, so I resolved to cut down in future to reduce my dependence. I'm now no more than a three-cup-a-dayer. But it is tough going sometimes as I sit at my desk. I've taken to drinking either herbal teas (see page 43), extremely weak China teas or occasionally decaffeinated coffee. Decaffeinated tea is available, too, for real purge enthusiasts.

How much caffeine are you having a day?

Coffee

The caffeine content of coffees varies enormously from type to type, brand to brand and even, where real coffee is concerned, by methods of brewing. Instant contains less caffeine, but may be consumed in greater volume. Where ground or beans are concerned, Robusta coffees have twice as much caffeine as Arabicas (the two most common species).

Average caffeine content per cup:
'Real' or ground coffee

Filter method	115 mg
Percolator	80 mg
Instant	65 mg

Tea

Tea contains more caffeine than coffee, weight for weight, but smaller quantities are used. However, a strong cup of tea-bag tea may contain more than a weak cup of instant coffee.

Average caffeine content per cup:

Average-strength tea	up to 60 mg
Cocoa and chocolate drinks per tumbler	4–5 mg
Cola drinks	30–60 mg

Roughly speaking, more than 300 mg of caffeine per day is higher than average intake.

There is a great trend at the moment for traditional drinks without ingredient X. Hence the boom in alcoholic drinks without the alcohol and caffeinated drinks without the caffeine. An astonishing 26 per cent of the population now claim to drink decaffeinated coffee sometimes and the grocery shelves are ready for us, with a host of different types of decaffeinated coffee beans, ground coffee, coffee filters, and instant coffee powders and granules.

Once, these doctored alternatives to the 'real thing' were thoroughly unsatisfactory substitutes, wishy-washy and characterless, but great technological strides have been made in the decaffeination process, with a resulting leap in satisfaction. But there's no getting away from it, decaffeination does take a certain something out – and you miss it, not merely in effect, but also in taste.

Caffeine itself is bitter, and although sceptics about coffee are concerned most with the 'bitter' quality, it is an integral and important element to the taste. Decaffeinated coffees are therefore milder, having less 'bite'. However it's not merely the caffeine that determines whether or not you get a good cup of coffee, the quality of the original beans and the level of roasting – whether it be low, medium or high – affects the end cup of coffee most. In general low roast = slighter flavour; high roast = more aggressive flavour.

According to Haydn Bradshaw, the Manager of Sensory Evaluation at Nestlé, one trick with manufacturing strong-tasting decaffeinated coffee is to increase the roast to give more edge and bite. Where instant decaffeinated coffees are concerned, because they tend to be milder, decaffeination leads to only a minor adjustment in taste.

Originally, chemical solvents (rather like dry cleaning fluids) were used to decaffeinate the moistened unroasted coffee beans. When the beans dried out, most of the solvent evaporated, although small traces were left. This method is still widely used although it has been somewhat superseded by two newer methods: the water method and the CO_2 method. In the water method, the beans are soaked in hot water, removing caffeine and some coffee. These elements are then separated by filters and the 'coffee' part is reabsorbed by the beans. In the CO_2 method, the caffeine (and nothing else) is removed from the beans using carbon dioxide in liquid form at high temperature under pressure.

The best decaffeinated coffee

When I conducted a tasting of decaffeinated 'real' coffees, both from beans and grounds for *Food and Drink* with Sid Hubbard, Chairman of the Coffee Trade Federation, we particularly liked Pure Kenya beans and ready-ground filter coffee from the Nairobi Coffee and Tea Company, decaffeinated by the Swiss water process (a variation on the water process) and Melroses beans and ground coffee. (Both are available in delicatessens; Melroses is also available in William Low supermarkets in Scotland.) Safeway's and Asda's filter ground also came out of the tasting well.

If you enjoy the taste of real coffee you should certainly go for 'real' decaffeinated rather than instant. And expert taster, Haydn

Bradshaw considers that beans are the tops, since absolute freshness is of such importance. The ideal is to buy small quantities from a local coffee merchant; grounds start to go off immediately and take only a day or two to go past their best, whereas beans stay fresh for longer (a couple of weeks, once roasted). Keeping either in the fridge or better still freezer, does retard the deterioration.

Most supermarkets sell a range of decaffeinated instant coffees, and they follow the pattern of 'regular' coffee, with powdered versions offering a milder (to my taste less convincing) taste than the more expensive granules.

When decaffeinated teas were first launched on to the market, they were greeted with some scepticism. We decided to test scientifically whether they actually had noticeably less effect on the body than ordinary tea, and posed our question to the Oxford Polytechnic. An experiment was set up and students were instructed to fast for twelve hours before acting as guinea pigs. Decaffeinated tea, made from a tea bag infused for three minutes was then brewed, and having drunk it down, the students were connected to spirometres, feeding them pure oxygen and monitoring their metabolic rate. There was little change before and after the tea.

Following exactly the same method, ordinary tea was then tested (and doubts were expressed as to whether any difference would be noted). But astonishingly a single cup of ordinary tea put the metabolic rate up by 15 per cent. There was a significant difference after all.

As a taster of teas, I am fully aware that my preferences do not reflect the general British taste. I like to drink tea so weak, it's almost transparent. Strong tea devotees complain that decaffeinated tea can lack that woomph they expect from a well-brewed cup; nothing I would complain about, I have to say – the less woomph the better, as far as I am concerned. As well as the two original decaffeinated teas first launched in health food shops, Luaka, (a mild blend of teas mainly from Ceylon) and the stronger St James's (made with African teas), Lyons decaffeinated tea bags are now also widely available.

EGGS AND POULTRY

INTRODUCTION
CHRIS KELLY

On 15 November 1988, I held in front of the cameras a government press release dated two and a half months earlier (26 August). A low-key warning entitled 'Salmonella and Raw Eggs', it read in part:

'In a small number of recent outbreaks of salmonella food poisoning, raw egg is believed to have been the cause of infection . . . The expert advice to the Department of Health is that it would be prudent for consumers, paticularly those who are more vulnerable, to avoid eating raw eggs or uncooked foods made from them . . . This advice applies only to raw eggs . . .' We spelt out, for the first time in public, what this meant to our cooking – no mayonnaise, no home-made ice-cream, no mousse, no licking of the cake mixing bowl and so on.

The government statement is notable for two main reasons. a) Because it was the first public announcement of the danger, despite the fact that as early as November 1987, Public Health Laboratories had reported to the DoH their suspicions that salmonella had spread to eggs. b) The press release concentrated solely on raw eggs, when we found evidence from the US that lightly cooked eggs could also be a problem – evidence which must, or certainly should, have been known to the DoH. Later we obtained a confidential Communicable Disease Report dated 30 December 1988 and compiled from Public Health Laboratory findings. This revealed a startling increase in the number of salmonella reports in 1988; that salmonella enteritidis (the strain particularly associated with poultry and their eggs) accounted for 55 per cent of those cases; and that '. . . a number of outbreaks of food poisoning due to this organism (s. enteritidis phage type 4) were associated with poultry and raw egg-based foods, *some of which had been lightly cooked.*'

In September 1988, the DoH spread the word (about raw eggs) to Environmental Health Officers and sent the same warning to hotels and catering establishments. Nevertheless, the vast majority of the public, and a great many professional food-handlers, were only made aware of the threat by our broadcast, weeks after publication of the DoH release. Conclusion? The message from the Ministry was crucially incomplete, and little urgency was displayed in its dissemination. For some considerable time most of us had been allowed to remain in ignorance of an epidemic.

The rest is history. Once our programme of 15 November had shown what the new advice meant for our cooking habits, the salmonella story gained astonishing momentum. By the following month the Chief Medical Officer, Sir Donald Acheson, finally advised that eggs for the elderly and sick, babies and pregnant women should be cooked until the yoke is solid. In December also, junior Health Minister Mrs Edwina Currie made her celebrated (and, for her, fatal) pronouncement: 'Most of the egg production in this country, sadly, is now infected with salmonella.' Two weeks later she resigned. Meanwhile egg sales had slumped by half. The Agriculture Minister, Mr John MacGregor announced plans to destroy 400 million surplus eggs and to cull four million hens. After Christmas his Cabinet colleague, Health Secretary Mr Kenneth Clarke, acknowledged that in 1988 the number of people infected by salmonella enteritidis had been 'about 12 000'. Some experts estimated that a more realistic figure might be anything between ten and a hundred times that many. In February 1989 the Government set up a Food Safety Committee to examine food hygiene from producer to consumer. Since then the shock waves initiated by *Food and Drink*'s original coverage have continued to ripple. Let us hope the Committee's eventual report both cleans up the poultry industry and restores our confidence.

In the meantime, one of the outstanding questions left by the affair is why didn't Environmental Health Officers get the Government's belated message across to catering establishments and their customers more effectively? The answer is they simply lack the manpower. Nationwide there are over 400 vacancies in their ranks, due, they say, to the inadequate number of training places in universities and polytechnics. At the time of writing, in the London borough of Camden alone, where there are more than 2000 food premises, there are posts for sixteen Environmental Health Officers in the commercial division, only four of which are filled.

To see for myself what the job entails I visited another of London's thirty-two boroughs, Barnet. There, as it happens, recruitment is not a problem. However, six EHOs are expected to

---

The facts about the scares

There have been a number of food poisoning scares in the past year. Here, in brief, is the current advice about salmonella and listeria:

Salmonella
Salmonella poisoning is growing rapidly. Its most common source is poultry and other meats.

Poultry
Over half our chickens contain salmonella and they must be cooked thoroughly to the bone.

Eggs
There is a small but proven danger from salmonella in hens' eggs. No-one should eat raw eggs; young children, the elderly, the sick and pregnant women should avoid semi-cooked eggs.

Listeria
Listeria poisoning is a tiny problem compared to salmonella, but listeriosis can lead to miscarriages, meningitis and even death.

Cheese
Soft-rinded cheese such as Brie and Camembert can contain listeria and should be avoided by pregnant women.

Chilled foods
Pre-cooked 'TV dinners' may contain listeria and should be re-heated thoroughly to a uniform 70°C (158°F) (or hotter). Obey standing times when microwaving.

Salads
Prepared 'greenleaf' salads can contain listeria and should still be thoroughly washed.

Above all do not cross-contaminate raw meat with cooked meat, whether by incorrect storage in the fridge, use of the same chopping boards and knives or failure to wash your hands.

(This advice was current in April 1989. It may have changed since. If in doubt consult your local environmental health office.)

---

deal with some 5000 commercial premises. When I was there a combination of illness and leave had so depleted the 'commercial' team that all inspections had temporarily ceased. (The non-commercial sector, incidentally, responsible for housing-related matters, is looked after by the residential division.)

Given the number of 'commercial' EHOs even in this comparatively fortunate authority, the brief seems to me to be over-ambitious. Barnet's Chief Environmental Health Officer, Geoff Fish, claims that its breadth makes for great flexibility. Probably true. However, it must also make for overwork and the sheer physical impossibility of covering all the ground regularly. Judge for yourself. The responsibilities of the six inspecting EHOs in the field include: food hygiene, inspection, registration, closure of food premises. Hospitals (now unprotected by Crown immunity) and related Health Authority premises. Food complaints, food sampling, bacterial quality, composition and labelling. Public houses; massage and special treatment establishments; pet shops; riding stables; dog breeding establishments. Health and safety at work; service of prohibition and improvement notices, inspection, accidents and dangerous occurrences. Pollution control: noise, water, wastes on land, dangerous substances, odour control, asbestos removal etc. General work: infectious diseases; drainage problems; sampling of water supplies; all planning applications and surveys (of commercial premises); health promotion schemes. Animal welfare: diseases of animals, farm problems. You'd need to be Clark Kent to cover even half of that.

Despite this workload an earthbound Terry Vaughan, a Senior Environmental Health Officer in Barnet, took a day off to inspect four premises and allowed me to act as observer. I was frankly shocked. Following a customer's complaint we called first at a small café. Conditions in the tiny back room were squalid. The cat fed in there and the walls were filthy. The flue was stuffed with a grimy tissue. In the food-preparation room the seal on the microwave was dangerously corroded. The temperature in the faulty fridge was twelve degrees centigrade (the agreed British Standard for the average temperature of fridges is five degrees). Grease-drips hung from the window bars. I was ready to believe Terry when he claimed that 'conditions generally, throughout the food trade, are appalling'.

Our next stop, a kosher butcher's, bore this out. In the backyard, where rats have been seen, the overflowing drain from next door had formed a grey, stinking river. Grease and filth were revealed beneath loose work surfaces. Congealed fat had accumulated on the chopping blocks. A cut on the proprietor's thumb bled through a grubby plaster. A packet of sausages in the cold-cabinet was three days past its sell-by date. 'I can see myself that we need some improvements,' said the distressed owner, 'but there isn't the money.' It was an interesting application of logic from someone whose own house was no doubt spotless.

A visit to the source of the grey river, a doner kebab shop, was equally depressing. Here uncooked meat sat beside part-cooked chicken in the cabinet, positively inviting cross-contamination. A nozzle oozing minced meat was inches away from a bag of garbage.

Finally we saw a sweet factory in a nearby basement. We found carpets used as work surfaces, greasy pans, and a metal tray for food preparation doubling as a bird-table.

Terry assured me that all four premises, chosen virtually at random, qualified for prosecution on several counts and that he would institute proceedings against at least two of them. He had taken dozens of photographs in evidence. The abysmal standards

---

Fridges and freezers

Recent surveys have shown that many of our fridges are too warm and that food-borne bacteria could easily multiply inside. The coldest point inside is at the bottom and the warmest at the top. The average temperature laid down by the British standard is 5°C (41°F). So your fridge should be no higher than 3 to 4°C at the bottom and 5 to 6°C at the top to achieve that average. If you are not sure whether it is functioning properly turn it to its coldest setting and when the milk begins to freeze back off slightly. Alternatively you can buy a fridge thermometer. Remember that such foods as meat and 'cook-chill' meals (ideal breeding grounds for harmful bacteria) are best kept in the coolest part of the fridge. Here are some other tips:

Defrost regularly and avoid ice build-ups
Check rubber door seals are not broken
Don't overload
Don't leave the door open longer than necessary
Don't put warm dishes in the fridge
Prevent any dust build-ups on the back housing
Don't place the fridge near a radiator or oven.

Freezers should be kept no higher than −18°C. At −9°C micro-organisms that can spoil food become active. You can also buy thermometers to check freezers.

---

we had witnessed were not at all unusual, he said. However, due to the pressures on Environmental Health Officers, conditions in low-priority businesses could remain unchecked for years. In some areas, they might (and do) escape inspection entirely.

It's true that prosecution can scare proprietors into radical improvements. It is, however, a comparatively expensive remedy; time-consuming and labour-intensive. Better by far to prevent, by education, rather than cure after the event. To this end, Barnet has introduced a six-hour training course for food handlers and publishes periodical guidance notes. The Environmental Health Department is also backing a national Heartbeat scheme which will sponsor awards to establishments offering healthier food choices, good standards of hygiene and no-smoking areas. Other environmental health offices around the country have recently started classes for people to learn the fundamental rules of food hygiene.

Nevertheless, at present staffing levels, our Environmental Health Officers are trying to push back Niagara. They are in the front line of the battle for health and hygiene on our behalf. They deserve our recognition and support. We must encourage, and where necessary reinstate, university and polytechnic training schemes; reminding the young, and ourselves, that the job is not merely worthwhile but absolutely, and increasingly, vital.

RECIPES
MICHAEL BARRY

Given the need to be careful with soft-boiled or undercooked eggs – though not for much longer, we all hope – it seems a good time to remember the pleasures of hard-boiled eggs. They have always been a favourite on rustic picnics, but they are also a delicacy on the hors d'oeuvre trays of *haut cuisine* and a treat from islands off the coast of Wales to islands in the South Timor Sea. Here are a cross-section of hard-boiled goodies.

PICKLED EGGS
Makes 12 pickled eggs

An old-fashioned treat still sometimes to be found in old-fashioned pubs. Properly made, a delicious and nutritious addition to all sorts of snack meals and high teas.

1½-pint (900-ml) preserving jar
12 hard-boiled eggs
1 pint (600 ml) cider vinegar
1 tablespoon white sugar
2 teaspoons pickling spice wrapped in muslin

Sterilise the preserving jar by boiling and then placing in a hot oven to dry, or using a disinfectant suitable for sterilising babies' bottles. Put the shelled hard-boiled eggs in the jar. Boil the cider vinegar, sugar and spices together until the sugar dissolves. When both the eggs and vinegar are cool pour the vinegar on to the eggs and seal the jar. Leave the eggs to pickle for 2 weeks before eating; they will keep for 2 months. Pickled eggs are a good addition to a ploughman's lunch and other salads.

TEA EGGS
Serves 4

Although eggs aren't what you instinctively associate with Chinese food, the Chinese have a host of recipes for them. This is often eaten as a breakfast dish or a snack, it looks lovely made with quails' eggs as a first course and served with some radishes, raw carrot and celery sticks. (Quails' eggs, of course, will only need 15 to 20 minutes boiling.)

6 hard-boiled eggs in their shells
1 tablespoon Chinese Kheemun tea

Crack the surface of the hard-boiled eggs all over using the back of a teaspoon. Place the eggs in a saucepan with enough water to cover, add the tea and bring to the boil. Simmer for 30 minutes. At the end of this time cool the eggs in cold water and peel. The surface will be beautifully marbled with a delicate hint of the tea. Serve with a salt and pepper dip, made by simply heating equal quantities of salt and freshly ground black pepper in a dry pan. This gives the pepper a highly scented flavour.

ANGLESEY EGGS

Serves 3 as a light meal

This is the recipe from the Welsh island I mentioned. A great luncheon dish, it is also very comforting for a cosy supper with lots of crisp, crusty bread to scrape up the juices.

1½ lb (750 g) leeks
1 oz (25 g) butter
6 hard-boiled eggs
1 pint (600 ml) bechamel sauce
2 tablespoons white breadcrumbs
2 tablespoons grated Parmesan cheese

For the bechamel sauce:
¾ pint (450 ml) milk
¼ pint (150 ml) single cream
1½ tablespoons plain flour
1 oz (25 g) butter
¼ teaspoon ground bay leaves
¼ teaspoon ground nutmeg
Salt

My crafty bechamel sauce is simply made by adding all the ingredients to the cold milk in a saucepan. Whisk the flour into the milk. Gently heat and stir, paying particular attention when the sauce begins to boil. Keep stirring and the lumps will disappear and you will have a shiny thick bechamel sauce.

Wash the leeks thoroughly, and cut into 1-in (2.5-cm) pieces. Gently sauté in the butter until just translucent, this will take about 3 minutes. Lay the leeks in a gratin or other heat-resistant dish. Cut the hard-boiled eggs in half horizontally and lay them on top of the leeks. Pour on the bechamel sauce and sprinkle with the breadcrumbs and cheese. Place under a hot grill for 2 to 3 minutes until hot and golden.

GADO GADO

Serves 4

A wonderful name for a wonderful dish from the Indonesian islands. You can make it with whatever vegetables you have handy; the only essentials being the salad greens (or blanched cabbage leaves), the eggs and the peanut sauce. Bean sprouts are a traditional addition.

1 crisp lettuce (or 12 blanched cabbage leaves)
4 hard-boiled eggs
4 new potatoes, boiled
½ cucumber, thinly sliced
4 carrots or 4 oz (100 g) green beans, trimmed, sliced and quick boiled for
5 minutes

For the sauce:
6 tablespoons crunchy peanut butter
1 tablespoon lemon juice
1 tablespoon brown sugar
1 tablespoon soy sauce
½ cup water

Slice the salad stuff into ½-in (1-cm) ribbons and arrange on a serving plate. Cut the eggs and potatoes into quarters and arrange them attractively; decorate with the cucumber and carrots or beans. Chill for 30 minutes. Mix all the sauce ingredients in a saucepan and bring gently to the boil. Don't panic, it becomes a smooth, shiny and scrumptious sauce to pour warm over the salad. Eat on its own or as part of a bigger South-East Asian meal.

VEGETARIAN SCOTCH EGGS
Serves 4
Good solid picnic or snack fare, you don't have to deep fry this as there is no raw meat to cook through. Easier and healthier in a hot oven!

6 oz (175 g) green lentils, soaked for 2 hours
1 onion
6 oz (175 g) wholemeal breadcrumbs
1 teaspoon sage
1 teaspoon thyme
1 teaspoon rosemary
1 raw egg
Salt and pepper
4 large hard-boiled eggs

Cook the lentils until just soft, about 30 minutes. Pre-heat the oven to 400°F (200°C), gas mark 6. Drain and purée in a blender or processor, then put in a mixing bowl and knead in all the other ingredients except the hard-boiled eggs. The mixture should be coherent, but soft. Adjust with the lentil cooking liquid to thin, or breadcrumbs to thicken the mixture. Dip the eggs lightly in flour and cover each with a quarter of the lentil mixture, working them round by hand. You can egg and breadcrumb them at this stage if traditional appearance matters to you. Put them on a greased baking tray and bake for 30 minutes until firm and lightly browned. Cool before serving.

SPECIAL SCRAMBLED EGGS
Serves 4

I am indebted to Elizabeth David for this idea (as for so many). She had the idea, I believe, from an Indian Army Officer who was also a great cookery expert. It does incorporate soft scrambled eggs, so if the all-clear hasn't sounded don't serve it to children, ill or very old people. The attraction by the way is in the contrast of textures as much as the flavours.

2 hard-boiled eggs
2 oz (50 g) butter
6 fresh eggs
Salt and pepper

Peel and chop the hard-boiled eggs coarsely. Melt the butter in a pan and scramble the fresh eggs gently until cooked but still soft. Fold in the hard-boiled eggs. Season and serve. Great on toast; sensational in pre-baked pastry cases.

EGG AND ANCHOVY MAYONNAISE
Serves 4

A simple but grand compilation that in the days when such presentation was fashionable would have been decorated with slices of truffle and slivers of peeled tomato and placed on the hors d'oeuvres trolleys of great restaurants. Easy and delicious to do at home.

8 hard-boiled eggs
8 tablespoons mayonnaise (preferably a 'light' one)
1 × 4-oz (100 g) tin of anchovies
½ red pepper, thinly sliced

Shell the eggs and cut neatly in half – a regularly dampened knife helps reduce 'drag'. Place the four halves face down in a flower pattern on each plate and spoon over the mayonnaise, decorate with the drained anchovy fillets and thinly sliced red pepper pieces. Chill briefly before serving.

MORNING AFTER EGGS
Serves 4

They say in New Orleans where this recipe originates that it was what was served to the young bucks after a night on the town to restore their energies before they returned to their wives. No comment on their efficacy, but they are delicious! Serve in long canoe-shaped pastry cases for authenticity or ramekins if you are feeling really crafty (or morning afterish).

1 red pepper, cleaned and thinly sliced
1 onion, sliced
1 clove garlic, chopped
2 tablespoons oil
1 lb (450 g) tinned tomatoes
1 teaspoon chilli sauce (tabasco or equivalent)
Salt and pepper
8 hard-boiled eggs, shelled

Fry the pepper, onion and garlic in the oil until soft. Add the tomatoes with a little of their juice and the chilli sauce. Stir and simmer for 20 minutes. Season with salt and pepper. Add the eggs and heat through before serving on a bed of the sauce.

ROYAL ICING AND ALMOND PASTE
As the Government recently advised us not to eat raw eggs due to the risk of salmonella, here are some alternative recipes for Royal Icing and Almond Paste, not using raw eggs.

Meri-White is a powdered meringue mix that can be used in place of egg whites in your cooking. Packets are available at Safeway, Presto, Asda and Waitrose, priced around 59p per packet; it can also be bought at sugar craft shops. If you have any difficulty in obtaining Meri-White contact the customer services department, at Manley Ratcliffe Ltd, Tower Road, Berinsfield, Oxford OX9 8LQ. It can be used for Royal Icing and Almond Paste. Alternatively you can use the following recipe for boiled Almond Paste recommended by Leith's School of Food and Wine:

1 lb (450 g) granulated sugar
½ pint (300 ml) water
Pinch of cream of tartar
12 oz (350 g) ground almonds
2 egg whites
1 lb (450 g) icing sugar (you may not need to use all of this)

Dissolve the granulated sugar and water over a low heat then add the cream of tartar. Bring the syrup to a boil until it reaches 240°F (115°C). If you do not have a sugar thermometer the sugar must reach 'soft ball' (the term used to describe sugar syrup reduced to sufficient thickness to form soft balls when dropped into cold water and rubbed between finger and thumb). Plunge the pan in cold water to arrest the heat, and stir in the almonds and egg whites. Return to the heat and stir until the mixture thickens. Turn out on to a board dusted with icing sugar, and begin to knead in the icing sugar until you have a workable paste.

CHICKEN RECIPES

The old chicken-and-egg dilemma leads me to a few chicken recipes, though here again the dreadful salmonella rears its ugly head. The pâté used to be made with the liver still a little pink to give a rosy coloured pâté. If you aren't sure about the provenance of the chicken livers you may want to cook them a little more thoroughly. Either way, it's delicious eaten with hot crusty French bread, grain mustard and gherkins.

CHICKEN LIVER PÂTÉ
Serves 4

Oil for frying
8 oz (225 g) chicken livers
1 clove garlic, chopped
½ teaspoon thyme
½ teaspoon marjoram
Salt and pepper
½ glass apple juice
3 oz (75 g) butter, melted
A couple of bay leaves for decoration

Heat the oil in a frying pan, add the chicken livers and fry until cooked. Add the garlic, thyme, marjoram and seasoning and cook for a further ½ a minute. Tip into a blender or food processor and add the apple juice and ¾ of the melted butter and process until smooth. Turn out into a ½-pint (300-ml) dish. Pour the rest of the melted butter over and decorate with the bay leaves. Chill in the fridge and eat within a day.

CHICKEN AND GRAPEFRUIT
Serves 4

There was (maybe still is, I'm not sure) a famous French 'Countess' whose party piece this was. It sounds an unlikely combination but is delicious and surprisingly different.

1 tablespoon oil
1 tablespoon butter
1 chicken, jointed into 8
4 tablespoons seasoned flour
2 pink grapefruits, peeled of all pith
Skin from ¼ grapefruit
Salt and pepper

Heat the oil and butter in a frying pan. Coat the chicken pieces in the flour, and sauté gently for 15 minutes until golden brown. Slice the grapefruit peel (with as little white pith as possible) into matchsticks. Drop the matchsticks into a small pan of boiling water for a moment, then drain. Divide the grapefruit into pegs and cut each in half lengthways. Add to the chicken and stir gently, simmer for 5 minutes, then add the blanched peel. Check for seasoning and serve with rice cooked plain or best, in a pilau.

SPICE ISLAND DRUMSTICKS
Serves 6

This is a super crafty recipe using store-cupboard ingredients – except for the chicken. It is great party food, especially to rescue the culinary side of those cooking catastrophes known as barbecues.

12 chicken drumsticks
6 tablespoons tomato ketchup
3 tablespoons Worcestershire sauce
3 tablespoons soy sauce
2 tablespoons made mustard (fresh or jar)
2 tablespoons oil
2 dessertspoons garlic salt
1 dessertspoon each basil, thyme and tarragon
1 teaspoon each cinnamon and ginger

Mix all the sauce ingredients together thoroughly. Coat the drumsticks, marinate for 10 minutes to 12 hours – the longer the better. Pre-heat the oven to 375°F (190°C), gas mark 5. Place the drumsticks on baking trays and bake for 45 minutes or until browned and sizzling.

CHICKEN FLORENTINE
Serves 6

In contrast to the previous recipe, this is a delicate and subtle chicken dish, equally good for simple suppers or grand dinners. It is called 'Florentine' because that is what the French call anything that has a significant amount of spinach in it.

1½-2 lb (750 g-1 kg) spinach (frozen leaf, or fresh)
1 stick celery
1 bay leaf
1 parsley stalk
A sprig of fresh thyme (optional)
1 onion
8 whole cloves
6 boneless chicken breasts

For the velouté sauce:
1 tablespoon butter
1 tablespoon flour
½ pint (300 ml) chicken stock (from cooking chicken breasts)
4 fl oz (120 ml) double cream
¼ teaspoon ground nutmeg
Salt and white pepper
3 tablespoons grated Parmesan cheese
2 tablespoons fresh breadcrumbs

Defrost frozen spinach and cook briefly, or blanch fresh spinach in boiling water for a minute, drain and squeeze out the excess water. To make a bouquet garni, cut the celery stick in half, place the bay leaf, parsley stalk and thyme on one half, sandwich together with the other half and tie with string. Peel the onion and stud with the cloves. Put these in a saucepan of water. Bring to the boil then add the chicken breasts and poach for 20 minutes. Make sure the chicken is thoroughly cooked and not pink in the middle.

Put the spinach in a gratin dish and lay the chicken pieces on top. Strain the liquid the chicken has cooked in and keep ½ pint (300 ml) to make the sauce.

To make the sauce, melt the butter in a saucepan, stir in the flour and cook for 30 seconds. Add the stock and whisk the sauce over a medium heat. It will gradually thicken as it boils. When a coating consistency is reached, turn down the heat and whisk in the cream, nutmeg and seasoning, cook for a few minutes more, then pour over the chicken. Sprinkle with Parmesan and breadcrumbs and place under a hot grill for 7 minutes until bubbling and golden.

STUFFED CHICKEN LEGS
Serves 4

In the 1988–89 series of *Food and Drink* Antonio Carluccio cooked Sunday lunch for the crew of Dowgate fire station in the City of London. He had been invited by their cook — fireman Keith Watt. Here is Antonio's recipe for stuffed chicken legs which the crew managed to eat in stages, between fire alarms!

4 whole chicken legs
4 thin slices of back bacon
3 tablespoons olive oil

For the stuffing:
2oz (50 g) fresh white breadcrumbs
2½ oz (65 g) Mortadella, cut into strips
A good pinch of nutmeg
1 tablespoon chopped parsley
1 oz (25 g) Parmesan cheese or mature Cheddar, grated
1 clove garlic, finely chopped
2 eggs
Salt and freshly ground black pepper

Take the legs, cut off any adjoining back bone and knuckles. With a very sharp small knife cut down the length of the bones on the inside and ease the flesh away, taking care not to puncture the skin. Your butcher could do this for you. Make the stuffing by mixing together the listed ingredients. Place a spoonful of this mixture in the middle of each rectangle of chicken. Fold the rectangle into a sausage-shaped parcel. Put a piece of bacon lengthwise along each parcel to close the join and flap over the end to close the parcel. Wrap kitchen string around the parcel to hold it together securely. Fry gently in a little olive oil until golden and crisp on the outside, and cooked in the middle. This will take 30 to 35 minutes.

CHRISTMAS SPECIALS

When Richard Shepherd and I answered the challenge to use left-over turkey in two minutes, we both looked to the East for inspiration. Both dishes I think would benefit from about a minute longer to let the flavours blend, but they *are* quick and easy. I have added a third idea for left-overs that takes a little longer.

The delicious Christmas pie is a crafty adaptation of several traditions for great pies containing a variety of poultry and game cooked and cooled to be eaten at Christmas. This one is simple and quite light but will feed a dozen people easily.

MICHAEL'S STIR FRY
Serves 2

4 oz (100 g) mangetout peas
½ red pepper, cut into thick strips
½ yellow pepper, cut into thick strips
5 spring onions, cut into 1½-in (4-cm) lengths
6 oz (175 g) left-over turkey, cut into strips the same size
and thickness as the peppers
1 teaspoon ginger powder
2 tablespoons hoi sin sauce
1 tablespoon cider vinegar
1 teaspoon brown sugar
1 tablespoon soy sauce
A little oil

The secret to a good stir-fry is a very hot wok or frying pan, and ingredients that are cut into roughly the same shape and size, to ensure even cooking. Heat the oil in the wok or frying pan. When really hot add the mangetout, peppers, spring onions and stir-fry for 30 seconds, then add the turkey. Stir-fry until the turkey is heated through, about 1 minute, then add the ginger, hoi sin, vinegar and sugar stirred into the soy sauce. Stir briskly, so that all the ingredients are coated in the delicious sweet-sour sauce and serve. This would be good served with boiled rice.

TURKEY AND WALNUT CROQUETTES
Serves 2

8 oz (225 g) turkey scraps (not skin)
4 tablespoons stuffing
4 oz (100 g) shelled walnuts
1 egg, beaten
4 tablespoons flour

Mince or chop the turkey meat finely – a food processor does this well. Mix thoroughly with the stuffing and the crumbled walnut pieces, then bind with the egg. Shape into sausages 2 × 1 in (5 × 2.5 cm), roll in the flour and shallow fry *gently* for 10 minutes until brown on all sides. Great with bubble and squeak for the perfect 'use it all up' left-overs meal.

CHRISTMAS PIE
Serves 12

A gamey pie to be eaten cold. Use two or three birds – chicken, pheasant and guinea fowl is a good combination. But any three will do.

2–3 birds: chickens, pheasant, guinea fowl

For the stock:
1 carrot
1 onion
1 stick celery
1 bay leaf
10 black peppercorns
Salt and pepper

For the shortcrust pastry:
8 oz (100 g) butter or margarine, cut into cubes
1 lb (450 g) plain flour
Pinch of salt
Cold water to bind

For the velouté sauce:
2 oz (50 g) butter
2 oz (50 g) flour
½ pint (300 ml) stock
½ pint (300 ml) single cream
4 oz (100 g) parsley, finely chopped

12 prunes, soaked to plump them up
Beaten egg with a pinch of salt to glaze

Put the birds and all the stock ingredients except the seasoning in a large pot or pressure cooker, cover with just enough water to cover and bring to the boil. Simmer for 1 hour until the chicken is very well cooked. Strain the stock, and remove the meat from the bones of the birds. Add the bones to the stock pot and boil again for 30 minutes. Season with salt and pepper. Remove the bones.

Make the pastry by rubbing the fat into the flour and salt. Add enough cold water to bind. Wrap in cling-film and refrigerate for 30 minutes. Roll out on a well floured board until ¼ in (5 mm) thick. Carefully line a 10-in (25-cm) spring-clip round cake tin. Gather the bits up and re-roll to make the lid and decorative cut outs.

To make the sauce, whisk the flour and butter into the stock and bring to the boil, whisking continuously. Add the cream and parsley and whisk again.

Pre-heat the oven to 350°F (180°C), gas mark 4. Fill the lined tin with a good layer of the cooked meat, add a few walnuts and prunes and the velouté sauce, repeat the layers, then put on the pastry lid. Press the edges down, make two slots in the lid to release steam and decorate with pastry leaves. Brush with egg glaze and bake in the oven for 75 minutes. Cool and then refrigerate for at least 4 hours before serving.

RICHARD SHEPHERD'S CURRIED TURKEY
Serves 2

1½ oz (40 g) butter
¼ small onion, very finely chopped
1½ oz (40 g) red and green pepper, very finely chopped
2 oz (50 g) button mushrooms, sliced
4 oz (100 g) left-over turkey, diced
1 teaspoon hot curry powder
2 tablespoons brandy
½ cup good double cream
Salt and pepper
Sprigs of parsley to garnish

Melt the butter in a saucepan or frying pan, add the onion and fry gently, add the peppers, mushrooms and turkey. Add the curry powder and cook for a further 30 seconds. If you are experienced with flambé you can flambé the brandy in the pan at this stage; if not, it could prove safer to simply add the brandy to the pan and carry on cooking. As the brandy reduces so will the hard alcohol taste. Next add the cream and stir until well mixed and hot. Season and serve in a warmed serving dish and garnish with sprigs of parsley.

CHRISTMAS TIPS

Here are a few tips for Christmas cooking and three recipes I picked up on my trip to America last autumn. Although they eat them in November in the USA – at Thanksgiving – that dinner is similar to our Christmas dinner here, in culinary as well as emotional terms. So try them at our Yuletide festivities.

COOKING TURKEYS

I have given this advice many times – but with the threat of salmonella it is well worth repeating.

If you are eating a frozen turkey this Christmas here are the best rules to follow. Defrost thoroughly. A turkey weighing 10 to 15 lb (4.5-6.75 kg) needs 4 days in a refrigerator to defrost thoroughly or 2 to 3 days in a cool place. To ensure the turkey is cooked thoroughly, allow 20 minutes per pound (450 g) and 20 minutes extra at 350°F (180°C), gas mark 4.

I also recommend that you cook the stuffing separately. You can add flavour to the bird by putting a lemon or peeled onion in the cavity.

Fresh birds *may* cook a little quicker. Test by putting a skewer into the top joint of the thigh. If the juices run clear with no 'pink' the bird is cooked through. If not give it 30 minutes more.

Don't forget to let it stand for 30 minutes after roasting, before carving, it won't get cold and won't crumble either!

STUFFING
Serves 6 to 8

4 oz (100 g) onion, diced
4 oz (100 g) celery
2 oz (50 g) butter
8 oz (225 g) white bread cut into cubes
½ pint (300 ml) water to moisten
8 oz (225 g) chestnuts, shelled and boiled, tinned or dried
(soaked, and simmered for 20 minutes)
1 egg, beaten
Juice of a lemon
A good pinch of dried sage
Salt and pepper

Fry the onion and celery in the butter until translucent, then combine with the rest of the ingredients. Turn into a buttered baking tray and bake in the same oven as the turkey for the last hour of its cooking.

AMERICAN THANKSGIVING GOODIES
I made a trip to New England last year at Thanksgiving. The fruits of my trip I heartily recommend for a British Christmas.

CRANBERRY RELISH
Makes 1½ lb/750 g
This relish is made in moments in a blender or processor.

1 orange, unpeeled – preferably unwaxed (organic)
12 oz (350 g) frozen cranberries
2 oz (50 g) shelled walnuts
5 oz (150 g) sugar

Cut the orange into quarters and depip. Put the cranberries, walnuts and orange pieces into a blender until roughly chopped but not puréed. Tip half the mixture into a bowl, sprinkle on the sugar, add the rest of the chopped cranberries and mix well. Leave for 2 hours to mature before serving; will keep refrigerated for 2 weeks.

OLD FASHIONED CRANBERRY SAUCE
Makes 1½ lb/750 g

8 oz (225 g) sugar
8 fl oz (250 ml) water
12 oz (350 g) cranberries

Bring the sugar and water to boil in a heavy-bottomed pan, add the cranberries. When they begin to pop cover with a lid and simmer for 10 minutes. Cool and refrigerate before serving.

CANDIED SWEET POTATOES
Serves 4

1 lb (50 g) sweet potatoes
2 oz (50 g) butter
1 tablespoon soft brown sugar
1 teaspoon cinnamon
½ teaspoon each salt and pepper

Scrub the sweet potatoes but do not peel. Simmer whole in a pan of water for 20 minutes until parboiled. To peel, rub the potatoes under cold water and the skins will fall off. Pre-heat the oven to 425°F (220°C), gas mark 7. Cut the potatoes into ½-in (1-cm) thick round slices and arrange in a buttered baking dish. Dot with butter, sprinkle with sugar, cinnamon, salt and pepper and grill or bake in a hot oven until the sugar is bubbling and the potatoes soft.

COURGETTE AND PEPPER PIZZA – PAGE 34

TEA EGGS – PAGE 51

TROUT IN DOUBLE ALMONDS – PAGE 79

STORM IN A TEACUP

HERBAL TEAS

JILL GOOLDEN

The thrilling arrival of the first tea leaves from the Far East in Eliza-bethan times probably provided a welcome change from down-ing endless herbal brews made from the produce of our local hedgerows and knot gardens. Sixteenth-century tastebuds felt they could do with a thrill and the stimulating infusion derived from *Thea sinensis*, rich in flavour, tannin and *kick*, provided just that, earning for itself such a following that over the next four centuries local-grown herbs found themselves relegated to the apothecary's repertoire.

Herb teas survived simply as medicines. 'I am sorry to say that Peter was not very well during the evening,' Beatrix Potter wrote in *The Tale of Peter Rabbit*. 'His mother put him to bed, and made some chamomile tea: and she gave it to Peter! "One table-spoon-ful to be taken at bed-time".' Modern medicine owes a great deal to the encyclopedic knowledge of the early herbalists, and some modern medicines, codeine for instance, are still derived wholly from plants.

In Britain there has historically been a resistance to taking things that 'do you good' purely for pleasure. They have been con-sidered less self-indulgent and much less likeable than those things that wantonly do you absolutely no good at all. But all this has changed over the past decade. And for the first time we have become obsessed with our health. Even our dearly beloved tea has taken a bit of a knock from the purists, and those in the business of peddling the 'healthier' alternative herbal teas are now reaping the rewards, with sales of herbal teas or 'tissanes' (made more from the hedgerows than the knot gardens, these days) increasing by up to 30 per cent each year since the early 1980s.

It's a booming business. Although not allowed to refer directly to the efficacious and curative properties claimed for these mysterious, many-coloured teas, strong allusion to their 'health-giving' properties are made in their names: Nervatea, Golden Slumbers, Bright and Early. There is even a book out called *The Healing Power of Herbal Teas* by Ceres. But against this fashionable healthy health store setting, the medical profession – never great upholders of what they see as 'alternative' cures – have taken a few swings at herbal teas, citing some ingredients to be downright dangerous.

Ginseng, of course, was bound up in an Olympic drugs scandal, but then ginseng always had the reputation for being the most risqué of the herbs . . . But others, too – simple things you'd find by the path on a country walk – have also been accused of being harmful in great quantities. So even committed advocates, such as Mark Evans of the National Institute of Medical Herbalists, author of *Herbalism – A Family Handbook* recommends you go easy on any one herb 'to avoid excessive pharmacological effect' and vary the basic ingredients of your teas drink to drink.

The classic way to make a herb tea is first to pick your herb . . . then to infuse it, like Mrs Rabbit, into a brew. Chamomile flowers have first to be dried before being infused; a comparison of the Real Thing with a tea bag version led my somewhat inexperienced buds to conclude that the bag is marginally preferable.

I had met the chamomile plant often in my childhood and had an aversion to its yeasty, weed-like smell – but I knew it (obviously erroneously) as ragwort. So when I was officially introduced to my first *bona fide* chamomile frond in the *Food and Drink* studios before the programme I was horrified. Having heard tell of the wonders of chamomile lawns, releasing a lovely scent at the prod of the deckchair leg, I had planted some seeds to grow in a corner of my pocket handkerchief garden. And to my horror, the area kept being plagued by miniature 'ragworts' (which, of course, I pulled up) while I awaited the first appearance of the fabled chamomile. That corner of the lawn is still looking expectantly bare . . .

In its pulverised tea bag form, I knew the flavour of chamomile only too well, probably like many other queasy expectant mothers. It had been the only drink I could take during two long pregnancies, and so now in times of slim unqueasiness, it's too reminiscent of those sickly times to be a favourite tipple.

Had I consulted *The Herbal* written in 1663 on which infusion I should have taken for morning (or in my case all day) 'sickneff', ironically I would have been on 'the iuyce of the greene leaues, branches and tendrels of the Vine'. Very appropriate!

I see that chamomile, which was recommended by old wives is, in *The Herbal*'s reckoning, 'good againft coldneffe in the ftomacke, foure belchings, voideth winde, and mightily bringeth downe the monethly courfes', which I could have done without. Modern herbalists recommend it for indigestion and to aid restful sleep.

Other essential 'herbs' tackled *en branche* yield (to me) more palatable potions. Peppermint is more retiring than you might expect, the mintiness saving itself until the final thrust of flavour. First sip, and it appears like a fresh, refreshing drink. *The Herbal* identifies that it is 'marvuellous wholefome for the ftomacke', good for watering eyes and 'taken inwardly againft Scolopenders, Bearwormes, Sea-fcorpions and ferpents' – so now you know. Modern peppermint tea bag literature promotes it as a counter to flatulence.

Elderflower, deemed to be good for colds, influenza and hayfever, has the powerful scent of a flower petal *pot pourri*. There's a slight hint of doctors' surgeries and damp wool there; but it tastes as though it's doing you the power of good, and is really quite palatable. Rose hips are, of course, a good source of vitamin C, and are believed to have constituents that combat diarrhoea, too. And they make delicious sweet, fruity, hedgerow-scented tea with an attractive sharp edge (derived from tannin), which you can apparently drink daily without fear of harm from overdosing.

The first herb teas to find their way into the supermarkets were derived from a single herb-type with chamomile leading the way, being quickly followed by peppermint and rose hip. The new wave, though, is for exotic blends of spices and herbs woven into single-bag elixirs with weird and wonderful names. And they are concocted with great imagination, a little bit of this and a tincture of that going to make a unique blend.

The best seller on the market is Orange Dazzler which boasts, 'Sip and let the sun shine'. It contains rose hip, hibiscus flowers, orange peel, blackberry leaves, cloves and orange juice. We served it, along with half a dozen mixed-herb competitors, to three studio guests to get their spontaneous comments. And they weren't hooked at first sip, it must be said. Professor Richard Lacey (of listeria fame) thought most of them tasted like 'ordinary tea with added poison'. His favourite didn't remind him in any way of tea (a plus, in his case): Rooibos Mixed Herb, consisting of rooibos (a South African caffeine-free black tea substitute), bramble leaves, vervain, liquorice, peppermint, cinnamon, chamomile and fennel. Its decidedly singular taste was described as 'positively disgusting, should be banned' by Dr Tim Laing of the London Food Commission. Conservative MP Sir Richard Body's favourite was Jackson's fruit cup, Lemon and Lime containing apple pieces, hibiscus flowers, rose hips, lemon peel, elderberries, orange peel, cinnamon and flavourings, which was popular all round.

Of course, Professor Lacey was only joking when he spoke of 'added poison', but what of the alleged harmful effects of herbal teas? At the time of writing, comfrey is the latest herb to get its come-uppance. *The Lancet* states that it contains toxic alkaloids which can be extremely harmful to the liver and suggests that the 'continued availability of comfrey products marketed as herbal teas must be questioned'.

Harvard Medical School carried out a survey of the naturally-occurring toxins in herbal teas and made the claim that 'twenty-six common herb teas are suspect and have already produced heart disease, skin disorders, stomach problems and injury to the nervous system' (*Self Health*). The culprit herbs implicated are comfrey (again), chamomile, nutmeg and two we do not see over here, the exotic sounding poke root and sassafras. *Self Health* asked Professor Shellard, Emeritus Professor of Pharmacognosy at London University to answer on behalf of the herbs. He admitted he would be unhappy about drinking comfrey tea, but said, 'As for chamomile, mint, lime and all the other common herb teas, there's no doubt about their safety.' So you can, within reason, experiment away.

Just a final word to those who tend to go at things immoderately, the *Which* bulletin sent fortnightly to doctors listed some 'potential unwanted effects' of herbs in medicines (and teas). *Taken in excess* liquorice can rarely cause oedema and hypertension; ginseng – hypertension and symptoms of hormone imbalance; chamomile, marigold and yarrow can cause dermatitis and allergy (caution to asthma sufferers); juniper – gastrointestinal irritation; and broom, tansy, pennyroyal oil and devil's claw should be avoided in pregnancy since they can cause miscarriage.

Talking of immoderation, I admit I've 'overdosed' on herb tea myself – in Madagascar. There, lemon grass grows everywhere, looking like a robust sort of reed tufting up under the coconut palms, and a bunch wound into a knot and put in a jug to be infused with boiling water makes a wonderfully refreshing drink. Nearer home, Waitrose sell lemon grass at 36p a pack, which makes a delectable infusion, too. You have to add the accompanying sound of the sea lapping the coral reef; and the hoot of the fruit bats and the click of the chameleons yourself . . .

Where to buy them

Herbal teas are widely available in health food shops and some supermarkets and cost from 3p to 7p a bag, with the blends of different ingredients being more expensive. Some shops sell bags individually, so you can afford to experiment.

The three blends liked best by our guest panel were:

Rooibos (not to everyone's taste) by Pompadour
25 bags for £1.05

Tropical Secret from Holland and Barrett
25 bags for 99p

Lemon and Lime by Jacksons
20 bags for £1.39

NEW FOOD FOR THOUGHT

INTRODUCTION
CHRIS KELLY

During the Second World War, accurate statistics were kept in Scandinavia on the incidence of heart disease. When the figures were analysed, researchers discovered a remarkable correlation. In the period of the German occupation, the number of heart disease victims declined sharply. And this was, obviously, at a time of intense stress; in itself a contributory factor to heart disease. When the invaders left, the line on the graph began to climb again. So what conclusion do we draw from the findings? Quite simply, scientists regard them as yet another indication of the links between diet and a healthy heart. For the most part, citizens of occupied countries had little or no access to fatty foods (fatty meats, butter and dairy produce in general, cakes, biscuits etc.). They must have relied largely on bread (if they were lucky) and anything they could glean from the land; unprocessed food rich in nutrients. No doubt it was monotonous and rarely satisfying but at least it lessened the risk of coronaries.

The experience illustrates two important points which Professor Michael Crawford, Head of the Nutrition and Biochemistry Unit at the Nuffield Laboratories of Comparative Medicine, is eager to stress. First, too much saturated fat is bad for us. Secondly, food that nature made (as opposed to food tinkered with by man), if eaten in balance, is good for us. Professor Crawford explained that the nutritional conditions during the five million years of human evolution 'set' human physiology. For most of that time what was available? Fish and seafood of all sorts; wild game; berries, nuts, seeds, leaves etc. Latterly man has intervened with techniques for 'engineering' some of our food. Professor Crawford believes the advances made by food technologists have been a mixed blessing. On the one hand he welcomes the increased availability of fresh fruit and vegetables for all seasons; on the other he deplores the fact that, in Northern Europe, we have developed a food and agricultural style which concentrated in the first instance on making animals fat. Because weight gain was the parameter used, the fatter the animals got the higher the price they fetched at market. So in effect what happened was that we were genetically selecting for obese animals. Next the food technologists developed high energy feeds and we stopped intensively reared animals getting any exercise, keeping them in stalls instead of fields ... 25 per cent of carcass fat, says the Professor, still ends up with four times as many calories coming from fat as from protein.

Bio-chemists, realising initially that butter was a scarce commodity, started using this surplus animal fat to make more affordable butter-lookalikes (margarines), thus adding a completely new dimension to the food structure. Thereafter science took an ever-increasing hand in food production and preparation, until now the bulk of our fat comes in invisible forms which we don't always recognise: biscuits, cakes, pastries, bread, sauces and pre-cooked dishes (fat helps to give them stability and to prolong shelf-life).

Professor Crawford reiterates that some aspects of this dimensional shift have been beneficial. There are indications, however, that others are potentially harmful. In an incredibly short space of time, measured against the evolution of mankind, human physiology has been forced to make unrealistically abrupt adjustments. Little wonder that our infinitely complex physical mechanisms regularly buckle under the pressure.

It seems then that we have quite literally become too clever for our own good. So where do we go from here? Short of dressing in animal skins and foraging for partridge and hazel nuts, like our remote ancestors, how can we re-establish a healthy diet and give our heart a fighting chance? (It's important to remember that diet is by no means the only contributory factor in heart disease. Others include smoking, lack of exercise, high blood pressure, heredity, obesity and stress.)

Research into the relationship between diet and heart disease provides us with many more questions than answers. There's a great deal we still don't know. There is, however, a scientific consensus on some items, so let's concentrate on those. The evidence available shows that a high intake of saturated fat is often linked with raised blood cholesterol levels. Cholesterol itself is essential to us: so essential that our liver manufactures it. Problems arise when we take on too much extra, via animal fat, or are unable to excrete the excess efficiently. Then cholesterol can clog up the arteries and reduce the flow of blood to the heart. This is why we're advised to cut down on saturated fats.

Nevertheless fats and oils, with the right qualities and quantities, are as vital to us as the correct levels of cholesterol. The basic building blocks of these fats and oils are called fatty acids. They come in three varieties: saturated, polyunsaturated and monounsaturated. Whereas saturated fat has a tendency to raise cholesterol levels, polyunsaturated fatty acids have a cholesterol-lowering effect. It's interesting that Greenland Eskimos and Japanese fishermen have a very low incidence of heart disease. It's thought the reason may lie in the special form of polyunsaturates found in fish – the Omega 3 fatty acids – which reduce the risk of furred-up arteries. Consequently a fish-rich diet (as long as it isn't swathed in batter or swimming in a thick cream sauce) is highly recommended. Hitherto monounsaturates were held to be neutral in the war against heart disease. New research, however, suggests they too are allies.

Another good ingredient in the menu for a healthy heart is the lowly oat, which on account of its soluble dietary fibre content has recently been given star-status. Dr Tony Leeds of King's College, London gave seventeen volunteers a carefully measured amount of oats as part of their daily diet over a period of seven months. The result was a 'fascinating discovery'. It showed that oats, as part of a low-fat, high-fibre diet, can help reduce cholesterol, though no-one is yet sure why. Similar reductions have been achieved elsewhere, notably in the United States where sales of oat products have subsequently rocketed. Dr Leeds is both wary of the Americans' over-reaction to the dangers of cholesterol, and to what they perceive to be the almost magical qualities of the cereal. He does, however, recommend that we eat some form of oats on a regular basis, as part of a healthy, nutritious diet. (In spite of the relatively greater claims made for oat-bran this can, if overdone, have a 'scouring' effect. Dr Leeds prefers wholegrain oats as they're eaten in porridge, for instance.)

From this welter of facts and figures, some useful guidelines emerge. I'm extremely grateful to Wendy Doyle, a research dietician at the Nuffield Laboratories, for her patience and co-operation in helping me enumerate them.

1   We should use all fats and oils sparingly and reduce saturated fats to a minimum (most are derived from animals e.g. hard cooking fats, dairy produce and visible fat on meat; coconut and palm oils are also high in saturates).

2   We should favour foods high in polyunsaturates (they may contain oils like walnut, corn, sunflower or soya) and monounsaturates (olive oil scores highly here – possibly one reason why Greece is at the bottom of the heart disease league-table). Some manufacturers have been slow to specify quantities on their packaging. We should put pressure on them to do so. Obviously if we don't know what's in a product we can't make a judgement.

3   We should eat plenty of fresh fruit and vegetables and other food rich in fibre, like wholemeal bread. There are even those who say a couple of glasses of wine a day are probably a good idea. It won't surprise you to learn that the leading authority in this line of research is a French scientist. Well, he would, wouldn't he? (See Chapter 7.) It's certainly true that France also has an enviable record on heart disease. Professor Crawford believes this may be partly because food is high on the French national agenda, which means that fresh, wholesome ingredients are *de rigeur*. To the British, all too often, a meal is just a refuelling stop.

Healthy heart facts

Professor Crawford and Wendy Doyle's conclusions are set out simply and clearly in a booklet. It is free from the following address:

Sanatogen Healthy Heart – Know Your Facts,
Food and Drink,
Freepost,
PO Box 21,
Godalming,
Surrey GU7 1BR.

Please send an A5 stamped addressed envelope with your request.

The list could be much longer. The World Health Organisation recently stressed, for instance, that heart disease starts with the mother and child and that mothers should breast-feed wherever possible.

In the end it's mostly a matter of common sense. Since we can't know the full implications of processing, it's best to aim for food and drink that's as close as possible to nature's intentions. As Professor Crawford reminds us, that's what we're designed for. A healthy diet may be only part of the overall picture, but it is at least an element over which we can exercise control.

RECIPES
MICHAEL BARRY

When you are concentrating on achieving a good balance of oils in your diet, don't forget fish. Fish oil is wonderfully nutritious and high in all the good – that is healthy – constituents.

TROUT IN DOUBLE ALMONDS
Serves 4

A delicious and ingenious way of getting as much nutty almond flavour as possible to contrast with the delicate softness of the trout. Your fishmonger will gut and clean the fish for you. Many supermarkets have fresh fish counters these days as well.

¼ pint (150 ml) milk
1 egg
Flour
2 oz (50 g) ground almonds
4 trout
1 oz (25 g) butter
A little oil
2 oz (50 g) flaked almonds
1 lemon

Beat the milk and egg together and put in a shallow dish or plate. Put the flour and ground almonds on separate plates. Coat the fish in flour then dip in the egg-milk, and finally coat with ground alm-onds. Melt the butter and a little oil in a frying pan and cook the trout, turning once. It will need approximately 3 to 4 minutes each side. For the last minute of cooking, add the flaked almonds to the frying pan and cook until golden. Serve with wedges of lemon. Try cooked cucumber as an unusual complement to the trout.

SAUTÉED CUCUMBER

1 cucumber, peeled
1 oz (25 g) butter
Salt and pepper

Cut the cucumber in half horizontally, and scoop out the seeds with a teaspoon to make a canoe shape. Cut the cucumber into 1-in (2.5-cm) pieces. Heat ¼ in (5 mm) of water in the bottom of a saucepan, melt the butter in it and add the cucumber pieces. Cook for 1½ minutes, season and serve.

TROUT EN PAPILLOTE

Serves 4

This is a French trick for cooking delicate foods so that all the flavour is kept in. You can make your *papillotes* (envelopes) the traditional way with waxed or greaseproof paper – or accept the advance of technology and use buttered aluminium foil. Either way, let each diner open the parcel themselves to get the maxi-mum benefit of the flavours that escape upon opening.

4 tablespoons butter
16 slices lemon
4 trout
Salt and pepper
4 tablespoons chopped dill or parsley
4 pieces greaseproof paper or foil 18 × 9 in (45 × 23 cm)

Pre-heat the oven to 375°F (190°C), gas mark 5. Use half the butter to grease the insides of the 'envelopes'. Season the fish, and place two lemon slices down the centre of each piece of paper, then the trout, then two more lemon slices, sprinkle over the dill or parsley, and dot with the remaining butter. Fold in the ends and then put the long edges together and fold over in 2-in (5-cm) pleats, making not a tight fish-shaped parcel but a slightly puffy rectangle. Place on a baking tray and bake for 25 minutes. Serve hot!

PICKLED HERRINGS
Serves 6 to 8 as a starter
Pickled herrings are a British tradition we have just about forgotten – the harsh astringent taste of rollmops are about all we have left of it. But this is subtle and delicate. Eaten with boiled new potatoes and good bread it makes a main course more than just a good starter. Ask the Scandinavians, who still eat them like this.

½ pint (300 ml) cider vinegar
¼ pint (150 ml) boiled water
1 carrot, peeled and sliced
½ onion, peeled and sliced
2 bay leaves
6 peppercorns
1 teaspoon salt
3 tablespoons sugar
8 herring fillets (sold as such or get your fishmonger working)

Put all the pickling ingredients in a saucepan and bring to the boil. Simmer for 10 minutes then cool. Pour over the herring and leave for at least 12 hours. They improve if left covered in the fridge for up to a week.

BAKED HERRINGS
Serves 4
The combinations in this may seem unexpected, but herrings lend themselves especially to a 'sweet and sour' treatment with their robust flavour and oily rich texture. Nicest eaten hot with boiled potatoes, this also is a good dish if there are any left-overs.

2 eating apples
1 large onion
8 herring fillets
Salt and pepper
½ teaspoon thyme
½ teaspoon marjoram
1 teaspoon paprika
2 tablespoons tomato purée
1 cup apple juice

Pre-heat the oven to 350°F (180°C), gas mark 4. Core the apples, peel the onion and slice both into ¼-inch (5-mm) rings. In an oval 2-in (5-cm) deep casserole, put a layer of onion and a layer of apple and then two or three fillets. Season with salt and pepper and sprinkle with the herbs. Repeat until all the ingredients are used up. Stir the tomato purée into the juice until blended and pour over. Cover loosely with foil and bake for 45 minutes. Uncover for the last 15 minutes of baking.

KIPPERS

I have talked about herrings – now for kippers. They are one of my favourite things. My tip for grilling is: place the kipper belly upmost under a hot grill for 3 minutes, then turn over for 3 minutes. Place a knob of butter on the belly if you like. You can also poach kippers gently in water or milk for 5 minutes. Grilling till crisp on the barbecue is another great idea. They are one of the few things I think an open fire improves (as well as the appetite, of course). But I also love kippers marinated. I first ate them like this at a do given by the Michelin Corporation in the foyer of what has become one of London's leading restaurants.

MARINATED KIPPERS
Serves 4

4 kipper fillets
½ onion, very finely sliced
4 tablespoons lemon juice
¼ pint (150 ml) olive or other salad oil

Skin the kipper fillets and cut into ½-in (1-cm) thick slices on the diagonal. Lay in a dish and cover with the other ingredients. Leave the covered fillets for 2 to 4 days in a refrigerator. This is a delicious starter or snack served with a sprinkle of black pepper on top and brown bread.

HERBED SALMON STEAKS
Serves 4

Though still a treat, salmon isn't the luxury item it has been for the last hundred years. Good and careful farming, especially up in the cleaner waters of Scotland, has produced delicious and economical fish. This recipe – though simply crafty – is still one of the all-time favourites for salmon. New potatoes and a cucumber salad – what more perfect for a sun-kissed evening?

4 salmon cutlets 1 in (2.5 cm) thick
1 tablespoon olive oil
2 tablespoons butter
2 tablespoons chopped parsley
1 tablespoon chopped chives
1 tablespoon lemon juice

Brush the cutlets with the oil and grill under a very hot pre-heated grill for 5 minutes on each side. Blend the butter, herbs and lemon juice together (a processor does this easily). Divide into 4 and place one quarter on each hot salmon cutlet. Serve quickly on *warm* plates.

HALIBUT IN ORANGE SAUCE
Serves 4

The dense, solid flesh of halibut is perfect for this recipe. You could use monkfish, but not a lighter, flakier fish such as cod. Serve it with a delicate rice pilau and a salad to follow.

1 tablespoon olive oil
4 × 6-oz (175-g) halibut steaks
1 tablespoon good soy sauce
8 tablespoons orange juice
Salt and pepper

In a non-stick pan or well seasoned frying pan, heat the oil and brown the halibut steaks on both sides. Turn the heat down, cover and cook for 4 minutes. Add the soy sauce and turn up the heat to sizzling. Turn over the fish and add the orange juice. Let it come to the boil and serve immediately, seasoning moderately on the plate. The sauce should be dark gold and syrupy.

CLAM CHOWDER
Serves 4

This was the chowder I was taught to make on Nantucket Island, Massachusetts, by a memorable cook and fisherman, Steven Bender. If you can't get clams, mussels make a delicious but different dish. Cook them closed, well scrubbed and discard the shells after they open. (American hardshell clams cost 20p to 40p each – if your fishmonger has none he can order them for you.)

8 oz (225 g) clams
1 large potato
2 tablespoons olive oil
1 large onion, chopped
2 spring onions, chopped
Small glass dry sherry
1 pint (600 ml) cream or milk
Salt and pepper

Open the clams and reserve the juice. Par-boil the potato and when cool enough to handle, dice. Reserve 1 pint (600 ml) of the liquid. Heat the olive oil and fry the potato and onion until the onion is translucent. Add the onion and potato to the clam juice and potato liquid. Add the spring onions, clams, sherry and cream or milk. Season and cook without boiling for 15 minutes.

OATS

I have never needed any encouragement to eat oats: a passion for porridge, a pleasure in muesli and a general fondness for their nutty, soft crunchiness has kept them part of my diet for years. Nice to know you are being smart as well as greedy, though, isn't it! The latest research suggests that oat bran is one of the most beneficial forms of fibre you can have in your diet.

MICHAEL'S MUESLI MIX

A home-made blend that varies depending on availabilities, but has one stable base. Keep it in an air-tight tin or box.

1 lb (450 g) medium oatmeal or porridge oats
4 oz (100 g) oat bran
4 oz (100 g) wheat flakes (or rye/barley flakes)
4 oz (100 g) raisins
4 oz (100 g) sultanas
4 oz (100 g) dried apricots, chopped
2 oz (50 g) walnuts, chopped
2 oz (50 g) Brazil or hazel nuts, chopped
4 oz (100 g) of a crisp almond or orange-based 'crunchy' cereal (optional)

Mix all the ingredients and serve moistened with fruit juice or milk, with your choice of plain yoghurt, honey or sliced fresh fruit. Yummy!

REAL PORRIDGE
Serves 2

With apologies to my Scottish friends whose grannies taught them. Use either porridge oats or oatmeal. The oatmeal takes about twice as long to cook but is nuttier.

3½ cups water
½ teaspoon salt
1 cup of porridge oats or oatmeal

Bring the water and salt to the boil. Stir in the oats in a steady stream, turn to a simmer and cook for 12 to 15 minutes, stirring every 4 minutes or so. Serve to your own taste – I'm afraid mine is 2 tablespoons of double cream, 1 tablespoon of soft brown sugar and to hell with the diet. (Only on Sundays, though, after a half kilometre swim.)

OAT AND POTATO CAKES
Makes 8

If you have any mashed potato left over, this is one of the most delicious ways of using it up. In fact, it's worth making extra for. It must be cold, though, before you begin. Traditionally made in little croquette shapes, I make these in patties which are easier to handle and just about as tasty.

1 egg, beaten
1 lb (450 g) cold mashed potato
6 oz (175 g) medium oatmeal
Salt and pepper
Sunflower oil for frying

Mash half the egg into the potato with a tablespoon of oats. Season generously. Divide into 8 and shape each one into a 2-in (5-cm) patty. Dip in the remaining egg and roll in the oats, pressing them well in. Leave to rest for 5 minutes before warming a *little* sunflower oil (a non-stick pan cuts down on the fat) and frying the patties until crisp on both sides.

BROCCOLI AND OATMEAL SOUP
Serves 4

This filling and unexpectedly textured soup combines the nutritional benefits of oats and broccoli. Can something this delicious also be good for you?

1 lb (450 g) broccoli florets
1 tablespoon olive oil
1 onion, peeled and chopped
Salt and pepper
4 tablespoons porridge oats
½ pint (300 ml) low fat milk
½ pint (300 ml) water

Trim the broccoli and reserve 4 small florets. Heat the oil and fry the onion for 2 minutes. Add the broccoli, cut in 1-in (2.5-cm) pieces, and season well. Add the oats and the liquids. Bring to the boil and simmer for 15 to 20 minutes. Liquidise, adding the reserved broccoli for crunch at the last minute. Check for seasoning and serve, if you fancy, with a dollop of natural yoghurt in each bowl.

OLIVE OIL

Olive oil, with its distinctive taste and solid body, needs using carefully in the kitchen. I prefer the golden oils of Greece to the green ones of Provence, and my favourite dishes reflect this eastern Mediteranean leaning. Either way these recipes should open the door to all those monounsaturates Chris was writing about.

CRISP FRIED AUBERGINE

Serves 2 as main course

Delicious as part of an hors d'oeuvres, or with a tomato and basil sauce as a vegetarian main course, the trick here is to drain thoroughly and cook hot and quick.

1 lb (450 g) aubergines
4 tablespoons cooking salt
8 tablespoons olive oil
4 tablespoons seasoned flour

Cut the aubergines lengthwise into ¼-in (5-mm) slices. Salt thoroughly and drain in a colander for ½ an hour. Rinse and pat dry. Heat the oil in a thick frying pan till almost smoking. Dip the aubergine slices in the flour and cook a few at a time until browned – about 1½ minutes a side. Drain on paper and serve as quickly as possible.

COOKED PEPPER SALAD

Serves 4

Cooking the peppers changes their flavour and texture quite remarkably. They become softer and sweeter – a real delicacy to eat with good crusty bread.

2 red peppers, de-pipped and halved
2 yellow peppers, de-pipped and halved
2 green peppers, de-pipped and halved
4 tablespoons olive oil
1 clove garlic, chopped
1 lemon
Salt and pepper
1 tablespoon chopped parsley

Slice the peppers lengthwise into ¼-in (5 mm) strips. Heat the oil in a frying pan with the garlic. Put in the peppers and fry gently for 15 minutes, turning regularly. Allow to cool, then squeeze over the lemon. Season and add the parsley. Mix gently (don't leave the oil in the pan – it gives and absorbs flavours) and pour into a serving dish. Cool and chill for 2 hours before serving.

STAYING LOW

ALCOHOL AND OUR HEALTH

JILL GOOLDEN

For centuries alcohol has greased the social cogs in Britain without being questioned. It's part of our way of life (and generally a very enjoyable part, too). Although the downside of excessive drinking has been obvious all along, it is only in the last few years that alcohol in all solutions and all quantities has come under scrutiny. Now a sufficient number of question marks have ineradicably been drawn beside the subject for us drinkers to question whether we should be doing it at all.

Visiting America when I was expecting a baby, I was horrified to find that their breakfast television (of which I had formerly been an addict) was interrupted by almost subliminal messages flashed upon the screen warning that imbibing any alcohol at all during pregnancy could seriously damage the unborn child. President Reagan's parting shot before leaving office was to sign an Act of Congress to force this warning on to the labels of all bottles of alcohol and into all bars in the shape of large signs. Bottles of all alcoholic drinks in the US are also, since November 1989 required to carry another wordy message reminding American citizens that 'Consumption of alcoholic beverages impairs your ability to drive a car or operate machinery, and may cause health problems.'

Unlike us, America has already, of course, seen full-scale prohibition and there is no doubt that a much more powerful anti-alcohol lobby exists over there than here. But the British press is increasingly crammed with reports of highly anti-social behaviour caused by excessive alcohol intake which begs the question 'Are things getting out of hand?'. Should we finally review our attitude to our most popular social prop? I, for one, neither want to drink more than is good for me, nor to encourage others to join me (in what I consider to be a delightful pastime) if it is going to put them at any major risk. So I set out to discover just where we all stand and what the experts – principally the medical profession – think we should be doing about our drinking habits.

To an extent, those of us who enjoy a drink with friends have probably been kidding ourselves. Look at a parallel situation; we don't every time we get behind the wheel of a car, think 'one small error and I could be maimed or dead'. At the back of our minds, we are dimly aware of this possibility. . . But how many of us think of the physical effects of just one more glass of booze? It would spoil the party, wouldn't it; though what we perhaps should be thinking is that it could spoil our lives.

'Alcohol can impair or wreck nearly every bit of the body,' Professor Griffith Edwards of the Addiction Research Unit of the Maudsley Hospital told me. He went on 'I'm not saying that it does so, but those are the risks we should live with.' He himself has not given up drinking, nor does he intend to. He knows what he is doing and simply exercises his own personal controls.

It used to be thought that small quantities of alcohol actually did the body some good, warding off heart attacks. Extensive research had revealed that it is not merely heavy drinkers who are more likely to suffer from heart attacks, but *non*-drinkers, too. Those least at risk were the light or moderate drinkers, so medical opinion agreed. But pow! Early this year an article in *The Lancet* shot this comforting theory to pieces.

New research, so the report went, showed that the high incidence of coronary heart disease in non-drinkers was attributable to the fact that many of them were reformed heavy drinkers who had become TT – possibly because of health problems – before the poll. Happily, I am able to report that medical opinion has still not conclusively agreed with the new theory.

The medical profession as a whole, the Department of Health and alcohol education groups are all agreed that there are 'safe limits' for alcohol intake, that drinking in moderation is unlikely to do you any harm and they have drawn up a simple, easy-to-follow guide for sticking within these limits.

> **'Safe limits' for alcohol intake**
>
> To monitor how much you are (and how little you should be) drinking, alcoholic drinks are categorised as units. All you need to remember is that each of the drinks below is a single unit:
>
> Half of bitter/glass of wine/small glass of sherry/single measure of spirits.
>
> Limits for 'safe drinking' have been set at:
>
> | | |
> |---|---|
> | 14 units a week for women | 21 units a week for men |
> | (equivalent to 2 drinks a day) | (equivalent to 3 drinks a day) |
>
> It is agreed you start to take risks with your health at:
>
> | | |
> |---|---|
> | 21 units a week for women | 35 units a week for men |
> | (equivalent to 3 drinks a day) | (equivalent to 5 drinks a day) |
>
> You could actually be doing yourself serious harm at:
>
> | | |
> |---|---|
> | 35 units a week for women | 50 units a week for men |
> | (equivalent to 5 units a day) | (equivalent to 7+ units a day) |
>
> The reason men have a higher tolerance is dependent not on their generally higher body weight, but on a difference in metabolism. The figures remain the same even for a woman of above average weight or a man of below average weight.

Our consumption of alcohol in Britain has risen dramatically over the last thirty years, with individuals now drinking twice as much as they were (although figures have admittedly remained static during this decade). And some of the consequences of more booze passing over bars and counters are worrying. According to Sir Bernard Braine, former Chairman of the National Council on Alcoholism, alcohol is implicated in half of all crimes, half of all cases of wife battering, half of all murders, two out of five fires, accidents at work, in the home, absenteeism from work . . . Startling figures, and sufficient for the Government to be nudged into investing £4 000 000 (twice their former commitment) over the next three years in education.

'Over the last couple of decades drink in real terms became much more cheap,' Professor Edwards of the Maudsley told me, 'and while we were worrying about an epidemic of heroin misuse, we actually had an epidemic of alcoholism of a sort that had not been seen since before the Great War.' That is not to say we are all included in this indictment; it still remains that most of us drink sensibly, while the few (among them large numbers of criminals and wife batterers) take things to excess.

Those of us who drink sensibly derive huge pleasure from a wide range of alcoholic drinks. As far as I am concerned, there is nothing in the non-alcoholic line to match the subtle deliciousness of wines, malt whiskies and some beers. I enjoy the taste, and let's face it, the effects, too. Alcohol is a marvellous relaxer and, in the right circumstances, pick-you-up as well. It has quite justifiably earned its important place in our lives. However, unless more drinkers exercise tighter controls on themselves – and indeed stick to the safe guidelines – we could see this pleasure condemned. And in the circumstances, justifiably so.

It isn't Government practice to dictate to individuals what they should or shouldn't do within the law. But there are those who would like to see a policy for alcohol, in the same way as we have a policy for sport. Sir Bernard Braine, for one, would like to see some restrictive regulations introduced and further provision made for education. He identifies the eighteen to twenty-four year-olds as the worst offenders and recommends the introduction of identity cards proving they are old enough to drink in pubs. Mind you, much of the publicity surrounding the problems of under-aged drinking exaggerates the situation, acording to Gellisse Bagnall of the Alcohol Research Group at the University of Edinburgh. Although in a comprehensive study of the subject she found that most thirteen year-olds had experience of alcohol, there seemed to be no correlation between early experience and later alcohol abuse.

It used to be imagined that you either had a weakness for alcohol, or you didn't; that excessive drinking leading to alcoholism was like a disease you might be unfortunate enough to contract. But it's not so. Alcoholic dependence is progressive. As a parallel, think of a bus route, with the first stop representing an individual's first drink ever and the terminus representing total alcohol dependence or alcoholism. The vast majority of adults in this country have boarded the bus, that is, they have had experience of alcohol. The majority also stay on the bus occasionally for one, two or even three more stops, and then they get off to do something else.

A few people board the bus and stay on board for a great number of stops, and repeat this habit so often that they begin to relate only to fellow travellers, considering those who have either never got on in the first place, or have travelled only a short distance, as being boring. Consequently they begin to ride on the bus all the time and before long, reach the terminus . . .

Another myth about heavy drinking is that people who drink a lot and never seem to suffer any ill effects, either at the time or the morning after, are not physically harming themselves. That is not the case at all; it's simply that they have taught their bodies to tolerate the superficial effects, including the visible signs of inebriation. But fundamentally their bodies are being affected in just the same way as if they had been showing signs of being drunk and suffering a hangover the next day. They are equally unqualified to drive and would stand just as much chance of failing a breathalyser test.

If these stalwarts were to stop drinking for a short time, their tolerance would soon drop, and the next time they had a boozing session, they would certainly know all about it . . . It's all to do with tolerance and dose. A simple way of controlling the amount you drink is to force your tolerance down by abstention and then to stick to the safe limits; just the same pleasant effects will be enjoyed on the reduced 'dose' of alcohol.

I'm constantly asked just how much I, personally, drink. People imagine because your job involves booze that you spend your whole time boozing, but I can assure you it's not the case. Tasting professionally, I taste the wine/beer/what-have-you – and then (unattractive though it seems) spit the mouthful out, and so absorb only minute traces of alcohol. So that means that, like you, I only drink socially and am able to stick within my fourteen units a week. If I feel like a drink, but don't want the alcohol, I may have an alcohol-free or a low-alcohol beer or cider, or a reduced-alcohol 'wine' (although the reduced-alcohol species aren't allowed to call themselves wine – in most cases with good reason). I reckon I have tasted virtually everything available on the market in this line, and have strong likes . . . and dislikes.

The most likeable class of low-alcohol drinks judged as a whole is, surprisingly, cider – dry cider is capable of yielding up its alcohol without either losing its appley flavour or becoming any sweeter. I was amazed to find whole orchards encapsulated in bottles of this delicious, thirst-quenching drink. Marcle Orchard by Westons (stocked by Waitrose) is my favourite, but to date, I've not found one I didn't like.

Beer in the form of lager and bitter, bottled, canned and occasionally on draught is the largest field in the low-alcohol line, and the best established in the market. But by no means is it the most consistent; there are some pretty boggy patches you could well stumble across if you investigate the area thoroughly. Probably one of the toughest tasting jobs I have yet tackled was to sift through all the 'LABs' and 'NABs' (Low-Alcohol and No-Alcohol Beers) on the market, both at room temperature (that's how you instantly sift the poor from the good) and chilled. The results of each blind tasting tallied, throwing up some clear favourites.

Of the lagers, two that have consistently done well in my blind tastings are Birell and Dansk, each seeming very 'pure' and natural, avoiding the sickly, cloying – sometimes very metallic – flavours of the 'also rans'. The bitter class contains as many disappointments, but two I particularly like are Whitbread White Label and Bass LA. All these have a little alcohol present – about 1 per cent. But if you want to avoid alcohol altogether, Kaliber is probably your best bet in the lager line and Smithwicks for bitter. These are both made by Guinness and to my taste buds have more than just that in common. Their similarities are enormous, with a darker colour and a malty whiff on the Smithwicks being the most apparent differences.

Beers with less than 1.2 per cent alcohol by volume are subject to the same labelling regulations as food, which means that unlike their stronger cousins, they must declare all the ingredients on the label. And this makes interesting reading, I can tell you. As you know, beers are supposed to be made from only four basic ingredients: water, malted barley, hops and yeast. There are frequently many more substances in the bottle than those alone, however. My tip for finding a good low-alcohol alternative to the real thing is to go for those products that stick most faithfully to the original recipe, keeping other additions to a minimum.

Many people, myself included, have reported completely unexpected hangover-type symptoms after drinking low-alcohol and no-alcohol beers – a tough penalty for 'staying low'. Looking into it, we discovered that although the inebriating alcohol is reduced in these drinks, the congener alcohols – those 'higher' alcohols often responsible in the first place for triggering off the symptoms of hangovers – remain at the end of the process, however low the apparent residual alcohol in the drink may be. Taking the alcohol out of alcoholic drinks is a new phenomenon and the technology is improving all the time. Let's hope this particular problem can be overcome soon, or I, for one, am going to be very cautious about LABs and NABs.

It's only fair to launch into the final class of reduced-alcohol drinks – wines – by saying that most of the really low alcohol examples are *foul*. Pity that, isn't it? It seems that wine is too delicate to sustain the process. Having a higher original alcohol content than either cider or beer, the alcohol itself is also a more intrinsic part of the flavour of wine and consequently dealcoholised wine becomes very wishy-washy and thin. There are, however, some reduced-alcohol grape products around that are delicious in their own way (all sweet, regrettably) – the slightly sparkling Petillant de Listel and Rosso and Moscato Vivace (all widely available) being excellent examples.

What is 'low'?

Whether you are drinking low-alcohol drinks for health reasons, or to stay within safe limits for driving, it is as well to know how alcoholic these new drinks are. Have a look at this chart, showing what percentage of a given quantity of beer is alcohol.

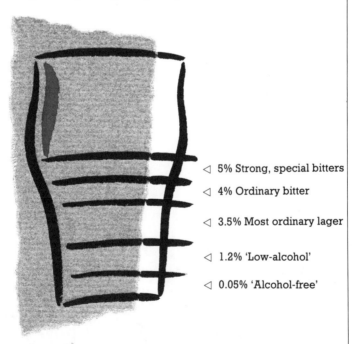

◁ 5% Strong, special bitters

◁ 4% Ordinary bitter

◁ 3.5% Most ordinary lager

◁ 1.2% 'Low-alcohol'

◁ 0.05% 'Alcohol-free'

As a point of comparison – red wines tend to be 12 per cent alcohol by volume, white wines about 11 per cent; port is around 18 per cent and gin, whisky and brandy, 40 per cent.

Remember that some premium, extra-strong lagers can be as alcoholic as some wines. And remember that 'low-alcohol' beers are about one-third the strength of ordinary lager.

But a word of warning here: look carefully at the label and you will see that there is still 3 or 4 per cent alcohol left in the drink – as much as there is in a cider or beer *before the alcohol is removed or reduced*. In my opinion, using the current dealcoholising methods, it is necessary for this alcohol to remain to keep the drink intact and permit it to retain the characteristics of wine. But of course it can still be intoxicating and still counts towards your weekly allowance of units, albeit in a more modest way, so watch out!

SUPERCOOK '89

INTRODUCTION
CHRIS KELLY

Our second Supercook competition, organised with the *Sunday Express* magazine, was an even bigger success than the first. There were more than 600 entries and standards were high. The top six were asked to make two courses (one of which must be a soup) for four people. The finals were held at Pru Leith's cookery school in London and judged by: Sophie Grigson, cookery writer; Michael Barry; and Michael Bateman, Deputy Editor of the *Sunday Express* magazine. The runners-up won luxury weekends for two at the Gleneagles Hotel, while the winner received a £10 000 kitchen and a promise from Baxters that they would can the triumphant soup and sell it commercially. Let us tell you about the semi-finalists and then let them describe their own recipes.

SEMI-FINALISTS

JOHN ANDERSON
John has lived in Penzance since the early 1960s. When he first went West there weren't more than a couple of good restaurants in the area. Now he estimates there are forty or so, including pubs. His favourite is The Riverside at Helford. This expanding market encouraged John to set up as an independent wine dealer, after 'taking the early bath' from the Navy, and teaching geography at a

school in west Cornwall. He's also the author of *Exercises in Pilotage*. Visits to France encouraged him to cook; he thought 'this is lovely but wouldn't it be nice to do it for a tenth of the price'. Perfecting the art of making his own puff pastry took three weeks; 'disastrous for the waistline!' His helper in Supercook '89 was a fellow member of the Royal Naval Auxiliary Service, Steve Harvey-James.

'The essence of these two dishes is style, sophistication and simplicity. They are luxurious, but apart from the salmon, relatively inexpensive. They are also reasonably foolproof.

'Any consommé demonstrates a chef's skills and this one is a limpid, sparkling soup with a heady aroma and powerful flavour, neither thin nor heavy.

'Koulibiac provides a heady combination of flavours and textures, the unctuous salmon/egg/prawn mix contrasting the astringency of the shallots and spinach to provide a truly memorable taste. But preparation is not complicated and once in the oven, one can forget it.'

MUSHROOM CONSOMMÉ
Serves 4

1 lb (450 g) mushrooms
1 tablespoon tarragon
2 tablespoons Madeira
Peppercorns
2 pints (1.2 l) chicken stock
1 tablespoon tomato purée
2 egg whites
Salt

Sweat the mushrooms, tarragon, Madeira and 4 peppercorns for 5 minutes. Then add ½ pint (300 ml) of chicken stock and the tomato purée and simmer for a further 3 minutes. Place in a blender and liquidise. Return to the saucepan, add the remainder of the chicken stock and simmer for 40 minutes. Remove from the heat and pass through a fine strainer twice, pressing the mushrooms to extract the last drop of flavour.

Place the 2 egg whites in a pan and slowly add the mushroom liquid, whisking constantly. When a crust forms on the surface, stop whisking and make a hole in the centre. Simmer for 20 minutes. Gently pour the consommé through a muslin filter, twice if necessary. Finally re-heat if necessary and add a tablespoon of Madeira, and salt to taste.

KOULIBIAC
Serves 4

14 oz (400 g) flour
Salt
6 oz (175 g) unsalted butter
Water to bind

For the filling:
1 lb (450 g) spinach, cooked
10 oz (275 g) smoked salmon
4 oz (100 g) rice, cooked
4 hard-boiled eggs, chopped
2 shallots, chopped
1 clove garlic, chopped
6 oz (175 g) prawns
Parsley, chopped
1 egg yolk

Pre-heat the oven to 400°F (200°C), gas mark 6. Make the pastry by rubbing the butter into the flour and salt until it resembles fine breadcrumbs. Add water to bind. Leave the pastry to rest for 30 minutes, then divide it in 2 and roll out each piece to an elongated shape. Lay the spinach, salmon, rice, hard-boiled eggs, shallots, garlic, prawns and parsley on one and place the second on top. Seal the edges and brush with egg yolk. Place in the oven and cook for 1 hour. I serve this with a purée of carrots, peas and cauliflower in 3 contrasting colours.

WILLIAM BANBURY

William lives in London. He spent twenty-seven years in the wine trade, both in London and Brussels, specialising in fine claret and Burgundy. He trained both in France and Germany. He has been interested in cooking from an early age: 'one followed one's mother in the kitchen'. He rates the cuisine of Sri Lanka very highly and once spent a holiday in Alsace looking for the best *foie gras*, only to discover that the *crème de la crème* was reserved for export. He rates himself an inventive cook, and says standards of British cuisine have improved enormously at every level. His favourite cookery writer is Elizabeth David. He was quite unfazed by the competition, though felt his fennel soup was not wholly successful. His helper was his niece, Louise Vaughan-Arbuckle.

'I have chosen a light vegetable soup to start with, as this will help to introduce the delicious Sea Bass that I have chosen for a main course. Fennel and chervil are the predominant flavours of my soup. Fennel was considered a symbol of success by the Ancient Greeks who called it "marathon" after their famous battle. It was popular in Shakespeare's time and was often used to flavour "sacke". It also goes very well with fish, and medicinally is a good digestive. Chervil is one of the most delicate aromatic herbs and is very good for the metabolism.

'Sea Bass is a most noble and sporting sea fish with a strong backbone and delicate flavour. I have chosen it en papillotte *to retain as much of its natural flavour as possible and serve it with Beurre Nantais, a sauce that is the pride of Normandy. Plain boiled rice is all that is required and a little salad as decoration.'*

CRÈME DE GUILLAUME
Serves 4

2 fennel bulbs (white parts only)
½ pint (300 ml) water
2 oz (50 g) butter
1 large Spanish onion or 2 small onions, peeled and chopped
2 leeks (white parts only), thinly sliced
1 tablespoon rice flour
2 large potatoes, peeled and thinly sliced
2 cloves
1 teaspoon salt
A pinch of white pepper
A pinch of grated nutmeg
1 bay leaf
1 in (2.5 cm) stem ginger (optional)
2½ pints (1.5 l) chicken stock
¼ pint (150 ml) double cream
Juice of ½ lemon
2 tablespoons freshly chopped chervil or 1 dessertspoon dried chervil
Chives or parsley, chopped

Wash, trim and chop the fennel bulbs, and place in a small saucepan of boiling salted water for 5 minutes. Remove from the stove and leave in the cooking water.

CHICKEN TIKKA, CRAFTY YOGHURT CHUTNEY, PARATHAS – PAGES 174–5

 VEGETARIAN COUSCOUS – PAGE 176

CHRISTMAS PYRAMID – PAGE 157

In a large saucepan, place the butter and onion. Replace the lid and allow the onions to sweat over a low heat until soft but not browned. Add the leeks, and allow to sweat with the onions for 2 minutes, stirring occasionally. Add a tablespoon of rice flour and cook as for roux blond. Add the fennel and the water in which it was cooked. Add the potatoes, the cloves, salt, pepper, grated nutmeg, bay leaf and ginger. Pour in the good chicken stock, stir, then bring to the boil and simmer for 40 minutes until the potatoes are soft enough to break up. Skim off excess fat. Remove the cloves and bay leaf, and put the rest into a liquidiser or pass through a fine sieve. Return to the saucepan, add the cream and lemon juice. Heat gently, but do not allow to boil. Place in soup bowls or a tureen and sprinkle with chopped chives or parsley.

SEA BASS AVEC BEURRE NANTAIS
Serves 4

1 very large bass or 2 medium or 4 small
5 oz (150 g) streaky bacon, thin strips blanched if too salty
Butter
Aluminium foil
2 oranges, thinly sliced
8 oz (225 g) shallots (reserve 4 or 5 for the sauce)
Thyme
Tarragon
Parsley
Marjoram
Salt and pepper
1 small wine glass brandy
1 small wine glass Madeira or sherry
1 lemon, sliced
4 oz (100 g) mushrooms, chopped

8 oz (225 g) long-grain rice

For the Beurre Nantais:
4 or 5 shallots (from the 8 oz (225 g) above)
Salt and pepper
1½ small wine glasses white wine vinegar
2 small wine glasses white wine
8 oz (225 g) unsalted butter
1 tablespoon finely chopped parsley

Salad to serve

Pre-heat the oven to 400°F (200°C), gas mark 6. Wash, gut and clean the fish. Cut the bacon into thin strips, fry gently in a little butter and drain. Place a sheet of aluminium foil in a shallow dish and place some orange slices and a little chopped shallot and herbs on it. Salt and pepper the fish, make a few slits in the skin and insert the bacon strips. Place the fish on the bed of oranges and pour over a glass of brandy and Madeira. Place the rest of the chopped shallot with some herbs and some slices of butter on top of the fish. Sprinkle with salt and pepper and lemon slices, and place a row of orange slices on the top. Top with chopped mushrooms. Fold the foil over the top and seal as *en papillotte*. Place in the oven and cook for 20 minutes.

Wash the rice and cook in boiling salted water in a covered pan.

To make the Beurre Nantais, chop 4 or 5 shallots and place in a saucepan. Add a little salt and pepper, the wine vinegar and white wine. Reduce until the shallots are cooked and almost all the liquid has evaporated. Remove from the heat and allow to cool. Then over a *very low* heat, whisk in the butter a knob at a time. When the sauce thickens to a rich opaque yellow, add a tablespoon of finely chopped parsley.

Remove the fish from the oven and serve with the boiled rice and Beurre Nantais and a salad of your choice.

LIZ COLEMAN

Liz recently moved to Lyminge, near Folkestone, in the Garden of Kent. Getting to grips with the local ingredients – including lamb, fresh vegetables, cider and wine – gave her an appetite for the competition. Her partly seventeenth-century house was also badly in need of a new kitchen. A map-maker by profession, Elizabeth now works as an administrative consultant to an insurance company. Cartography, she maintains, has helped her develop the patience a good cook needs. A lover of old British recipes, she recently came across one for Sussex Bailiff's Bliss – shortcrust pastry containing ground almonds, eggs, walnuts and glacé cherries. For Supercook '89 she was partnered by her brother-in-law, Phil Ranner, whose wife was so close to giving birth, he was permanently glued to a portable telephone throughout.

'Having recently moved to Kent, I created the soup using local ingredients, of which the wine is one. It makes a good hearty quantity and is just right for cold damp days. Although I do not skin the apples, the skin cooks into the soup and amalgamates with the other ingredients.

'The Chicken "Portfolio" is an invention of necessity! One dinner time the only ingredients in the fridge were drumsticks, mushrooms and smoked ham. A jar of spiced apricots from my company's Christmas hamper (hence the name!) and some cider were also available, so I set to!'

APPLE AND LEEK SOUP
Serves 4

1½ oz (40g) butter
1 lb (450 g) leeks, cleaned and sliced into rings/semi-circles
3 average-sized eating apples (Cox's), cored and chopped (but not peeled)
A pinch of mace
Freshly ground black pepper (I do not cook with salt, but put a salt cellar on the table for those who would like it.)
2 cloves
½ pint (300 ml) Kentish cider
1½ pints (900 ml) good stock (preferably lamb)
To finish, about a dessertspoonful of whipped or soured cream per serving

Melt the butter in a heavy pan and add the chopped leeks and apples with the mace, pepper and the cloves and sweat until soft. Add the cider and stock, bring to the boil and simmer for about ½ an hour. Using a hand blender, liquidise the soup in the pan. This soup should not be thickened or sieved. Re-heat if necessary and serve in warmed bowls with a spoonful of cream floating on top.

CHICKEN PORTFOLIO
Serves 4

4 large chicken drumsticks
4 thin slices of raw smoked ham
4 spiced apricot halves (from a jar of Harrod's spiced apricots or home-produced sweet-pickled apricots)
2 tablespoons olive oil
4 (approx) shallots (depends on size), skinned and sliced
4 oz (100 g) mushrooms, wiped and sliced
¼ pint (150 ml) white wine (from the Staple Vineyard, Kent)
¼ pint (150 ml) (or more if required) chicken stock
Plain flour for dusting plus about a tablespoonful for the roux
Freshly ground black pepper

Bone the chicken drumsticks and open them out. On each drumstick lay a slice of raw smoked ham and an apricot half. Roll them up again and tie with fine string into a neat parcel. Dust each parcel with seasoned flour. Fry the parcels in the olive oil until they are browned all over. Take them out of the pan and keep them warm. In the pan fry the shallots until soft and add some sliced mushrooms. Sprinkle in some flour off the heat and make a sauce in the pan with the wine and chicken stock. Replace the chicken parcels and simmer gently for an hour or so, turning the parcels occasionally.

DUCHESSE POTATOES
Serves 4

1 lb (450 g) potatoes
Butter
Grated nutmeg
1 tablespoon soured cream
Brown breadcrumbs

Four people will require about a pound of potatoes – four largish potatoes is about right. Peel them and cut them into similar-sized pieces and put them into a pan to boil for 12 to 15 minutes depending on the variety. Pre-heat the oven to 400°F (200°C), gas mark 6. Drain and purée the potatoes with an electric mixer, adding a good knob of butter, a grating of nutmeg and tablespoonful of soured cream. Put the potato mixture into a large forcing bag with a star nozzle and pipe in whirls on a well greased baking tray. Sprinkle some brown breadcrumbs on top and put into the oven for about 15 minutes.

CARROTS AND BROCCOLI
Serves 4

1 lb (450 g) carrots
8 oz (225 g) broccoli florets

I like to peel and cut local carrots into fingers about 3 in (7.5 cm) long and to boil them for about 10 to 15 minutes (depending on variety and age). On the top of the carrot pan I would set a steamer containing the broccoli florettes, which would take about the same time to cook.

RUNNERS UP

BERNICE CLARKE

Bernice lives at Hurst Green in the Ribble valley. Married to an architect and with a three-year-old daughter, Catherine, Bernice began to be fascinated by cooking in the kitchen of her aunt's Blackpool hotel. She enjoyed 'musseling with a large bucket on the beach. You can't do that now.' She lived in Earl's Court for two years: 'only having two gas rings and a grill challenges anyone'. She is unequivocal about the main influence on her cooking: 'If you can read, you can cook with Robert Carrier'. She also admires Delia Smith. She enjoyed the semi-final but thought the final was 'horrendous. The pressure really got to me. I sat and watched it with a cushion on my head.' She would like to learn West Indian cooking. Her assistant was her husband, David.

'We are privileged to live in a rural location in Lancashire and our recipes have been devised to present a truly appetising meal which could be enjoyed with relish on returning home on a damp, dark winter's evening from recreational or work activities.

'The basic premise is that the meal should fulfil all of the following criteria:

1 *Be simple;*
2 *Be nourishing;*
3 *Be moderately low in cost.*

'Our intention has been to utilise as many ingredients as possible that are locally obtained direct from the English countryside, or from the English kitchen garden. We estimate an overall cost of £3.00 per head for the meal and we feel that providing it was well prepared and presented it would satisfy the appetite of King Henry VIII.'

BROAD BEAN AND BACON SOUP
Serves 4

Make a light ham stock in the traditional method. If more flavour is required add approximately 3 oz (75 g) smoked bacon in one piece (soak to remove excess salt). Reserve the meat from the ham hock or pestle. Ensure the stock is fat-free.

4 oz (100 g) butter
8 oz (225 g) onion, finely chopped
¼ pint (150 ml) sherry
½ lb (225 g) potatoes, chopped to the size of the beans
1½ lb (750 g) broad beans, after shelling
1½-2 pints (900-1200 ml) stock
Salt and pepper
Sage, freshly chopped

Melt the butter in large pan and sweat the onions for approximately 10 minutes until golden brown. Add the sherry and potatoes and beans. Cover with a double thickness of damp greaseproof paper, replace the lid and simmer for approximately 40 minutes. Add the stock. Remove to a blender or processor, and process until the soup is a liquid consistency. Repeat as many times as necessary. After each process, put the soup through a fine sieve into a clean pan, using a soup ladle to speed up the process of pressing the vegetables through the sieve. Discard all the vegetables left in the sieve. Re-heat and season as required. Prior to serving, add the chopped meat from the hock and garnish with freshly chopped sage.

GLAZED PHEASANT
Serves 4

1 brace pheasant
2 eggs
4 tablespoons cooking oil
½ cup honey (English preferred)
4 tablespoons lemon juice
4 tablespoons paprika
1 teaspoon salt

Pre-heat the oven to 350°F (180°C), gas mark 4. Cut the pheasant carcasses lengthways in halves, or quarters if preferred. Arrange in a greased baking dish. Beat the eggs, add the remaining ingredients and mix well. Spoon over the pheasant pieces and place in a moderate oven for 45 minutes. During cooking, turn and baste the pheasant pieces frequently with the honey sauce. Increase the oven heat to 400°F (200°C), gas mark 6 during the last 10 minutes to give the pieces a crisp brown skin. I like to serve this with orange and watercress salad and parisienne potatoes.

LYN KENNEDY

Lyn was born in Timmins, Ontario, close to Hudson's Bay; a former goldmining town and the last stop on the line. She read English and Psychology at the University of Western Ontario. When she set off to see Europe, she got a job as a social worker in Edinburgh and decided to stay. While there, she ran two antique shops, and now lives in Auchtermuchty with her husband. In Canada 'we canned everything in sight, ready for the winter'. In Scotland, fresh sea fish and 'exotic fruit and vegetables from Europe' were a revelation. On the programme we mistakenly said she enjoys 'hurling'. Lyn was amused: 'I don't hurl, I curl.' Baxters were impressed with her chutneys and may develop them commercially. Lyn's helper was her sister-in-law, Jean.

'The subtle flavour of the Jerusalem artichoke attracted me to try to do something that would add to it without losing its character. There is no onion or leek used in either the soup or the stock to detract, and I feel the pheasant complements and marries nicely.

'Venison is often too richly treated with herbs and red wine. Here, moistened with white wine, it can stand on its own with the flavour accentuated by the use of root vegetables – carried over into the accompanying dishes of roots and nuts.'

CREAMED JERUSALEM ARTICHOKE WITH PHEASANT
Serves 4

For the stock:
2 cooked or uncooked pheasant carcasses
6 pints (3.4 l) water
2 teaspoons salt
1 bay leaf
½ teaspoon peppercorns
1 small carrot, sliced
2 sticks celery, chopped
A few sprigs of parsley

2 lb (1 kg) Jerusalem artichokes, peeled and sliced
1 teaspoon lemon juice
Salt and white pepper to taste
2 pints (1.2 l) pheasant stock
2 oz (50 g) potato flour
6 oz (175 g) pheasant meat
¼ pint (150 ml) single cream
3 tablespoons chopped fresh parsley

To make the stock, place all the stock ingredients in a deep saucepan and cook slowly for 1 to 1½ hours. Drain, then return the liquid to the saucepan. Cool the pheasant pieces to make handling easier. Remove the meat from the bones and reserve. Return all the ingredients to the liquid. Cover and cook slowly for 1 to 1½ hours.

Prepare the artichokes by cooking in a small amount of boiling water to which 1 teaspoon of lemon juice has been added. Cover and simmer for 10 to 20 minutes until tender. Drain thoroughly, then purée in a food processor.

Strain 2 pints (1.2 l) of pheasant stock into a saucepan and add the artichoke purée. Gently heat and season to taste. Thicken with the potato flour added to a little water. Add the pheasant meat and cream, heating gently. Garnish with parsley. Serve with freshly made Oatmeal Bannocks.

BRAISED VENISON CHOPS
Serves 4

For the marinade:
1 cup dry white wine
1 medium onion, sliced
1 carrot, sliced
1 celery stalk, sliced
½ teaspoon salt
½ teaspoon whole peppercorns
¼ cup white wine vinegar
1 clove garlic, crushed
1 bay leaf

4 venison chops
4 oz (100 g) butter
1 tablespoon flour

Place all the marinade ingredients in a bowl and marinate the chops for 1 to 2 hours. Strain and reserve the marinade. Place the chops on the strained vegetables in an ovenproof dish and pour in ½ cup of marinade. Brush the chops with butter. Heat a grill to very hot (or pre-heat the oven to 475°F (240°C), gas mark 9). Cook the chops until brown, then turn and brown the other side. Reduce the heat to half and cook for a further 20 minutes. Remove the chops to a warm platter. Add the remaining marinade to the pan juices and vegetables. Strain and skim off the fat. Thicken with a flour-water mixture and pour over the chops.

SCALLOPED TURNIP AND APPLES
Serves 4

½ medium turnip
1 tablespoon butter
1 large cooking apple
3 tablespoons brown sugar
Pinch of cinnamon
2 tablespoons all purpose flour

Peel, dice and cook the turnip in boiling water. Pre-heat the oven to 350°F (180°C), gas mark 4. Drain and mash the turnip, adding the butter. Peel, core and slice the apple. Toss in the brown sugar and cinnamon. Arrange in alternate layers in a casserole, making the top and bottom layers turnip. Top with the flour and knobs of butter. Bake in a medium oven for 30 to 40 minutes.

CHESTNUT POTATO CROQUETTES
Serves 4

8 fresh chestnuts
1 lb (450 g) potatoes
2 oz (50 g) butter
2 eggs
Salt and pepper
Flour

Pre-heat the oven to 350°F (180°C), gas mark 4. Peel and roughly crush the chestnuts. Boil the potatoes then mash them. Dry them off by beating in the pan over a low heat. Remove from the heat and beat in 1 oz (25 g) of butter. Separate the yolks from the whites of the eggs. Beat the yolks one at a time into the mashed potatoes. Season to taste. On a well floured board, divide the potato mixture into 8, roll and shape into croquettes. Flour them well, then dip them in the lightly beaten egg whites. Finally roll then in the raw chestnut pieces. Place in buttered ovenproof dish and brown for 15 to 20 minutes at medium heat.

THE WINNER

DAVID WILLIAMS
From Parkgate, South Wirral, Cheshire, David is a submarine production manager for Cammell Laird, currently building the third

of the Upholder class which will be called HMS *Ursula*. He says of his interest in cooking: 'I can only say it developed'. An avid viewer of *Food and Drink*, he saw the competition advertised and said to himself: 'I can do that'. He was right. In the semi-final he cooked Welsh lamb marinated in five gallons of home-brew. His soup used an ingredient for which Parkgate is famous – delicious brown shimps. He was fascinated by visits to Baxters, who are canning the soup commercially. Favourite cookery writer? 'Elizabeth David. It almost seems dangerous when you read it – so off the norm – but exciting.' The judges particularly liked the fact that in David Williams' dishes the flavours were paramount, and put him first. The reaction to his victory at work was 'absolutely tremendous'. His helper: David's eleven-year-old daughter, Julie, an expert shrimp-peeler!

'Parkgate on the River Dee is renowned for its shellfish, cockles, mussels and particularly shrimps, fished by two families going back six generations.

'My first course is "Parkgate" Fish Soup which has a delicious stock produced from the shrimp shells and must not be overpowered by other strong flavours. My recipe has been developed and adjusted to suit the family critics.

'My second course is lamb. The one small family butcher in the village kills his own Welsh lamb, which he buys young and fattens on his salt pastures. The lamb is full of flavour and succulent.'

FISH SOUP
Serves 4

1¼ lb (500 g) whole white fish (whiting) or 1 lb (450 g) white fish fillets
3 pints (1.75 l) water
1 pint (600 ml) shrimps in shells
1 clove garlic, peeled
A knob of butter
2 teaspoons paprika
½ onion, roughly chopped
1 lb (450 g) mussels in shells, bearded and scraped
½ lb (225 g) cockles in shells
1 dessertspoon tomato purée
Fresh parsley, finely chopped or 4 tablespoons single cream (optional)

For the bouquet garni:
½ bay leaf
Spring of fresh lemon thyme (ordinary thyme is too strong)
Parsley stalks
Stick of celery
6 peppercorns
Above wrapped in leek leaves

Gut the fish, remove the head, fillet and skin. Put the head, skin and bone into the stock water. If fillets or fish pieces are used, skin and place the skin and scraps into the stock water. Dice the fish flesh in ¾-in (2-cm) cubes and put to one side. Shell the shrimps, place the shrimp shells in the stock water, bring the stock to the boil and simmer. Rub a frying pan with the garlic and fry the fish cubes in the butter with the fresh paprika. Cook for about 5 minutes until the transparent appearance of the fish turns opaque white. Put on one side.

Place the onion in a saucepan with a cup of water and bring to the boil. Place the closed mussels and the cockles into the saucepan, close the lid and cook for 8 minutes. Remove the onion and shells, and reserve the shellfish and stock. Remove the stock from the heat and pass through a sieve. Let the stock settle for 5 minutes. Decant the stock from the residue and return to the heat. Add the bouquet garni. Boil until the stock has reduced to 1¼ pints (750 ml). Add the fish, cockles, mussels, stock and tomato purée, and simmer for 5 minutes. Remove from the heat and add the shrimps. Sprinkle with very finely chopped parsley and serve, or swirl a tablespoon of single cream in each bowl. Personally I don't.

LAMB WITH ROSEMARY SAUCE
Serves 4

½ saddle of lamb 2-2½ lb (1-1.25 kg)
1 bottle Claret
1 tablespoon fresh rosemary
Black pepper

For the rosemary sauce:
2 oz (50 g) butter
1½ oz (40 g) plain flour
½ pint (300 ml) red wine
Milk
4 teaspoons fresh finely chopped rosemary

The ½ saddle of lamb should be at least 5 days old with dry skin. Slice the fat with cross diagonal cuts not quite through to the flesh. Marinate for 24 hours in red wine with a tablespoon of rosemary which has been bruised. Pre-heat the oven to 425°F (220°C), gas mark 5. Place the lamb under a hot grill for 10 minutes each side. Season the lamb with milled black pepper. Place the lamb in the oven and cook for 45 minutes. Remove the lamb from the oven, stick rosemary twig ends in a line along the joint for decoration. Cut the meat from the 'T' bone and slice thinly. The lamb should be pink.

For the rosemary sauce, make a basic roux with the butter and flour. When cooked, add ½ pint (300 ml) of red wine from the marinade and cook until thickened. Add a little milk to achieve a pouring consistency. Put 4 teaspoons of the chopped rosemary into a mortar and pestle and grind. Add 1 tablespoon of the sauce to the mortar and continue grinding to achieve a paste. Stir the paste into the sauce and serve with the lamb.

Gratin Dauphinois made with Desirée Potatoes is a natural accompaniment of lamb. I particularly like it with carrots cut into thin sticks and tied into bunches with chive stalks. Cook for 10 minutes with a knob of butter and ½ cup of water in a sealed saucepan.

THE FINALISTS' MAIN COURSES

In the final, the three finalists repeated their soups for the judges and cooked one, new main course recipe. Here's what they came up with.

DUCK WITH LIME SAUCE
Serves 4
Cooked by the winner, David Williams

1 × 5 lb (2.25 kg) duck
1 bay leaf
6 peppercorns
1 pint (600 ml) water
Salt
2 tablespoons honey
Ground black pepper
Knob of butter
2 limes
2 tablespoons white sugar
For decoration: 1 green apple, 1 grapefruit, 2 tablespoons cointreau, 1 lime

Remove the duck breast by cutting down each side of the breast-bone. Snip through close to the wing joint. Cut the legs from the carcass and remove the bones. Put the leg bones only, the bay leaf and peppercorns and water into a saucepan and simmer till reduced by half. Strain.

Sprinkle the duck pieces with salt, grill each side on high until brown, (not more than 4 minutes). Prick the skin and grill for another 2 to 3 minutes. Spread the joints with honey and season. Melt the butter in a heavy pan and gently fry the duck for about 3 minutes each side. Keep it warm. Remove the zest from the limes, cut into fine shreds, then squeeze out the juice and reserve. Add the sugar to the pan juices. Heat until caramelised. Add the stock and boil until reduced and syrupy. Stir in the lime juice and half the shredded zest.

Cut the apple into balls with a melon baller. Soak, with the grapefruit segments, in the cointreau (or use lemon juice).

Slice the duck and arrange on a heated plate. Pour over the sauce and scatter with the remaining lime shreds. Top with apple, grapefruit segments and lime wedges. Serve with broccoli and potatoes.

ROAST CHICKEN WITH HERB STUFFING
Serves 4
Cooked by runner up Bernice Clarke
Due to the risks of salmonella from undercooked poultry we advise you to stuff only the crop end of your chicken and not the body cavity. Bernice Clarke made patties with the left-over stuffing which she baked on a well-greased baking tray.

For the stuffing:
3 tablespoons olive oil
2 tablespoons butter
4 oz (100 g) minced veal
1 medium onion, grated
3 oz (75 g) fresh breadcrumbs
1 tablespoon chopped or dried tarragon
2 tablespoons chopped fresh parsley
Zest of 1 lemon
A pinch of cayenne pepper
Salt and pepper
1 egg, beaten
4 tablespoons dry white wine

4 lb (1.75 kg) chicken

Melt the olive oil and butter in a frying pan, add the veal and onion and fry until golden. Add the breadcrumbs and herbs and fry with the meat. Add the lemon zest, cayenne and salt and pepper to taste. Mix the stuffing well and allow to cool. The chicken and the stuffing should be the same temperature before the bird is filled. When the stuffing is cool, mix in the egg and wine. Stuff the bird. Weigh the bird after stuffing and allow 15 minutes to the pound (450 g) in an oven at 425°F (220°C), gas mark 7. To test if the chicken is thoroughly cooked pierce the thigh with a sharp knife, if the juices that run out are clear it is done, if they are still pink cook for a further 15 minutes.

FISH PIE

Serves 4

Cooked by runner up Jean Kennedy

For the haddock filling:
12 oz (350 g) haddock poached in a Court Bouillon made from:
2 pints (1.2 l) of water
½ pint (150 ml) vinegar
1 carrot, sliced
1 onion, sliced
1 stick celery
12 peppercorns
2 bay leaves
2 tablespoons salad oil
Salt

For the salmon filling:
12 oz (350 g) salmon
Court Bouillon

For the white sauce filling:
1 oz (25 g) butter
1½ oz (40 g) flour
¼ pint (150 ml) milk
¼ pint (150 ml) single cream
Salt and pepper
1 tablespoon finely chopped capers
1 tablespoon finely chopped chives
1 tablespoon finely chopped parsley

For the spinach filling:
½ lb fresh or frozen leaf spinach
2 tablespoons butter
1 small onion, chopped
1 clove garlic, chopped
Salt and pepper
¼ teaspoon ground nutmeg
1 egg, separated

For the scallop and prawn filling:
4 scallops, cut in half lengthways
6 large shelled prawns, cut in half lengthways

For the pastry:
11 oz (300 g) plain white flour
5 oz (150 g) wholemeal flour
1 teaspoon salt
Grated rind of 1 lemon
1 oz (25 g) dried yeast
1 egg
3 tablespoons olive oil
7 fl oz (200 ml) lukewarm water

To make the haddock filling, simply boil all the Court Bouillon ingredients together for 20 minutes, cool slightly, add the fish and poach until white and firm, about 6 to 8 minutes. When cool, bone and flake.

To make the salmon filling, poach the salmon in the same Court Bouillon as the haddock for approximately 4 minutes until cooked. When cool, bone and flake.

For the white sauce, melt the butter in a saucepan, add the flour and cook for 30 seconds. Whisk in the milk and cream, and stir as the sauce thickens. Season and add the finely chopped herbs.

To make the spinach filling, steam the spinach or cook in a covered saucepan in just the water used to wash the leaves. Melt the butter in a pan and fry the onion until translucent, add the garlic and fry gently. Drain the spinach and put in a blender or food processor, add the onion, garlic, nutmeg, seasoning and egg yolk, and whizz until smooth. Beat the egg white until stiff and fold into the spinach mixture.

Pre-heat the oven to 400°F (200°C), gas mark 6. Sift the flours and salt and add the lemon rind and yeast. Add the egg and olive oil and mix, then add the water and work together. Roll out two-thirds of the pastry on a floured surface and line an 8- to 9-in (20- to 23-cm) spring-form cake tin. Prick the base. Fill the pastry case with the flaked haddock and cover with the white herb sauce. Smooth over the spinach mixture and arrange the raw scallops and prawns on top. Next put on the layer of flaked salmon. Brush the pastry rim with beaten egg and roll out a lid with the rest of the pastry. Crimp the edges closed. Brush the top with beaten egg, make a steam hole, decorate with pastry leaves and leave to rise for 15 to 20 minutes before baking for 45 minutes.

MAKING THE MOST OF MEAT

INTRODUCTION
CHRIS KELLY

BRINGING HOME THE BACON

There is no more emotive item on the British menu than bacon, even though we're eating much less of it than we used to (5.42 oz each per week in 1987, as against 7.24 oz in 1957). Despite the decline, we still consume around £430m worth of the stuff every year, 90 per cent of which is produced by intensive farming methods. And there's the rub. Most of the bacon we buy today simply doesn't compare with the rashers we remember from childhood. At least that was the gist of a great many complaints we received in the *Food and Drink* office. Here's a typical example from Mrs Marilyn Marland, who lives at Bowdon in Cheshire:

'. . . I cannot find a decent piece of dry bacon anywhere. It's all wringing wet and excruciatingly salty. When grilled or fried it ends up lying in a puddle of grey brine. Quite disgusting . . .' Now as it happens I was born in Cheshire, and I'm happy to confirm that in days of old (well, not all that old!) the local bacon was gloriously tasty.

In order to test the validity of our viewers' criticisms, we arranged a blind tasting of twenty-one bacons from a variety of sources. There were five Dutch bacons (Holland is now our main foreign supplier) under supermarket own labels; ten branded British bacons; two branded Danish bacons; and four traditionally cured home-grown bacons. In each case we selected unsmoked back, since the smoking process can hide a multitude of inadequacies.

Marilyn Marland was an obvious choice for our panel of judges. She was joined by another disgruntled correspondent, Eileen Durham from Cumbria (who actually works in a super-market), and an old friend – Ken Clements, a former master butcher.

It was hard to believe that so many products purporting to be the same thing could taste so very different. Flavours ranged from bland, through fishy, to succulent and delicious. Textures and appeal varied widely too, though most were at best uninspiring and at worst downright unpleasant. We know from our research that some modern breeds, cheap feeds and brine-based curing systems have all contributed to the bland, watery rasher in our shops today. At the end of the marathon session, by a unanimous verdict, the winner was a bacon with matchless flavour and just the right amount of fat, which did not shrivel in the pan. The pro-ducer of this paragon? The Real Meat Company, based at Warminster in the West country. Its bacon is grown as nature intended – without the aid of growth promoters, pre-emptive drugs or additives in the feed – and cured by one of the traditional methods. And just to emphasise that the result was no freak, the bacon in second place was also reared and cured in an old-fash-ioned way – dry salted by Maynard Davies of Weston under Redcastle in Shropshire.

THE REAL MEAT COMPANY

It's a measure of the emotiveness I mentioned earlier that the Real Meat Company's triumph on television was immediately followed by two thousand requests. One desperate viewer, too impatient to wait for the *Food and Drink* fact sheet, got the company's number from directory enquiries on the night of transmission and placed an order there and then. Richard Guy, who founded the organisation with his wife, Gilly Metherell, says the response obvi-ously meant 'there's something terribly wrong with British bacon'. So how have he and Gilly set about getting it right? I drove down to Wiltshire to find out.

East Hill Farm, Heytesbury, where it all started, lies in the lee of a firing range owned by the Ministry of Defence. On red-flag days, jet fighters scream across the rolling landscape pretending it's enemy territory. The pigs rooting on the steep slopes seemed blissfully oblivious.

When Richard and Gilly – a former commodity trader in grain – opened for business here in 1986, they were driven by a mutual desire to produce meat of the highest quality. Moreover, they were determined to do so with two paramount considerations: every step would be taken to promote the welfare of their animals, and at no stage would growth promoters, additives or non-therapeutic drugs be used. (In intensive production, continuous medication is routine. Richard used a human analogy to explain why: 'If you stopped the overcrowded 8.30 at Waterloo and kept everyone inside for three months, they'd all have pneumonia after a week.' Unless you kept on dosing them, that is. No-one knows what effects these artificial aids may have on future generations. With a nine-month-old daughter, Frances, Richard and Gilly are not prepared to take any chances.)

Helped by an animal charity – Compassion in World Farming – they drew up a strict code of practice. Among other things it stipulates that:

1 Pigs cannot be kept in intensive systems. There will be no tethering or constant-crating of sows; no tail cutting or castration of piglets. All pigs are straw bedded for comfort and to allow 'rooting'.

2 Calves are reared by natural suckling and kept outdoors except in hard weather. No market trading of young calves.

3 Poultry is allowed access to range when old enough and when climate permits. No wing-clipping or any other form of mutilation is allowed.

4 Lambs are reared by natural suckling.

5 Abattoirs are carefully monitored and those failing to meet the company's requirements are not used.

The code is applied equally stringently to the numerous other farms which now supply the Real Meat Company. As far as beef is concerned, for instance, Richard estimates that only one in perhaps two hundred potential herds satisfies his criteria. We visited an outstanding example – Norridge Farm, Warminster, intriguingly owned by an Austrian millionaire. Here the quality and well-being of the cattle was perfectly obvious even to my amateur eye. Similarly at East Hill Farm itself, the care and attention given to the pigs and table-chickens is extremely impressive. The latter are housed in warm, dry, daylit sheds with plenty of room and access to the great outdoors when they're old enough. Compared with their relatives in intensive conditions – up to five per square foot, never allowed out and very often under artificial light twenty-three and a half hours a day, to make them eat more and fatten faster – these birds are in clover.

While the animals clearly benefit from humane treatment, so,

Bringing home the bacon

The two winning bacons in the *Food and Drink* tasting were:

1 The Real Meat Co. It has its own shops and other companies also supply their meat. For a list write to them at:
East Hill Farm,
Heytesbury,
Warminster,
Wiltshire BA12 0HR.
For orders, contact them at:
Real Meat Direct,
Deverill Road Trading Estate,
Sutton Veny,
Warminster BA12 7BZ
Telephone: 0985 40501.

2 *Maynards Farm Bacon,*
The Hough,
Weston under Redcastle,
Shrewsbury,
Shropshire SY4 5KR.
Maynard Davis does not supply other shops but he does have his own farm shop.

Since our programme many supermarkets have begun to stock traditional, dry-cured bacon. Other good, traditional bacons are obtainable from:

Old Spot Farm Shop,
Piltdown,
Near Uckfield,
East Sussex TN22 3XN.

Sandridge Farmhouse Bacon,
Sandridge Farm,
Bromham,
Chippenham,
Wiltshire.

Heal Farm,
Kings Nympton,
Umberleigh,
Devon EX37 3TB.

---

of course, does the consumer. The fact that the chickens live in stress-free conditions, consume additive-free feed and are given almost twice as long to grow as the intensively-farmed equivalent, means they have exceptional flavour and tenderness; as do the other items on the Real Meat Company's ever-growing list.

To witness the regime at East Hill Farm and its satellites is to realise, with absolute clarity, that this is the ideal way to raise live-stock for the domestic market decently and responsibly. How-ever, it's pointless pretending that quality of this high order comes cheap. The system is 'ludicrously labour-intensive' says Richard Guy. Consequently the product – from pork and lamb right through the scale to cheese, ice-cream and free-range eggs – sells at a premium (on average, probably 20 per cent more than the intensively-reared alternative). Nevertheless the indications are that large numbers of customers are able and willing to pay it. At the time of my visit (March 1988) the company was turning over £1.25m per year (with a retail value of £2.5m).

Because of heavy labour costs, increasing demand will only reduce prices marginally by saving money on transport. So we have a choice to make. Do we care enough about our health, and that of the animals we consume, to pay extra? Are we prepared to make a sacrifice in order slowly to reverse the factory approach to farming, which has become so entrenched over the past twenty years?

If we are, then we must put pressure on our supermarkets to stock the goods we want. Beehive in Cambridge have got the message and are giving the Real Meat Company's products a try. In the meantime these are also available at the company's own shops in Bath, Chelsea, St John's Wood and Sutton Veny, and at some twenty-eight other retail outlets, though only as far north as Leicester. If you live further afield, however, don't despair. In addi-tion, the company operates an efficient overnight delivery service to any location on mainland UK. (See information box.)

RECIPES
MICHAEL BARRY

Making the most of mince meat is a good subheading for this chapter. Mince, of whatever meat, is often looked down on as the cheapest cut there is. It is certainly true that in many countries, especially peasant ones where they had little meat, what there was was pretty old and tough, so mincing was the solution. Lasagne, moussaka, keema curries, chilli con carne – recipes, in fact, from all over the world which rely on mince – testify to this, the oldest tenderisation process. But the dishes that emerge are often delicious and typical of their region. Here are three of them, starting with what is practically the national dish of America, Meat Loaf, often eaten on Sunday lunchtimes and flavoured according to the national origins of the American family concerned. You serve it in slices with the appropriate vegetables for a great meal.

US MEAT LOAF (ITALIAN STYLE)
Serves 6

Try serving this loaf with pasta and a sauce. This Italian style sauce would go well:

1 lb (450 g) minced beef
1 large onion, finely chopped
4 oz (100 g) breadcrumbs
2 cloves garlic, chopped
A pinch of thyme
A pinch of oregano
1 heaped tablespoon chopped fresh parsley
1 heaped tablespoon grated Parmesan cheese
2 teaspoons tomato purée

For the sauce:
1 pint (600 ml) passata or drained and chopped tinned tomatoes
1 lb (450 g) mushrooms, sliced
1 clove garlic, chopped
A pinch of basil
A pinch of thyme
A pinch of oregano
Salt and pepper

Pre-heat the oven to 425°F (220°C), gas mark 7. Mix all the ingredients except the tomato purée and cheese together thoroughly and turn into a 2-lb (1-kg) loaf tin. This is only used as a mould and should be turned upside down on to a baking tray. Give it a good tap and lift off. Spread the top of the loaf with tomato purée and sprinkle on the cheese. Place in a hot oven for 45 to 50 minutes.

To make the sauce, simply heat all the sauce ingredients together until the sauce reaches simmering point, simmer for 5 minutes then serve.

STUFFED PITTA BREAD
Makes 6

From the Middle East, pitta bread has become commonplace in our high streets. It makes great home-made meals as well. This delicious snack or light meal is, however, a very dangerous recipe. I've never been able to make enough. If your grill can take three or four slices, a family party can devour them and regain its appetite by the the time the next batch is ready. Beware, and make plenty!

1 lb (450 g) minced beef
1 medium onion, very finely chopped
1 tablespoon tomato purée
2 tablespoons freshly chopped coriander or parsley
1 teaspoon allspice
1 teaspoon cinnamon
A little oil
Salt and pepper
3 pitta bread, sliced open into 6 leaves
Parsley or coriander leaves to decorate

Look at the opened pitta bread: you are going to cover the crumb or bread-like side. Lightly toast the pitta bread under the grill, this will stop it going soggy when filled. Mix all the ingredients together and spread a thin layer of mince on to the pitta, covering the entire surface. Grill for 5 minutes and serve. You can decorate the pitta with some chopped parsley or coriander leaves.

HUNGARIAN GOULASH SOUP
Serves 6

The food of middle Europe – Hungary, the Balkans, Czechoslovakia – is a pretty unknown quantity to us. But it has its own strong and strongly flavoured traditions. One of the few recognisable dishes that has made the journey is goulash. Even in its homeland it is a very variable dish. What I've suggested here is a soup version, wonderfully warming and welcoming on a chilly night.

1 lb (450 g) minced beef
1 onion, chopped
1 tablespoon paprika
1 tablespoon caraway seeds
A pinch of thyme
A pinch of marjoram
1 lb (450 g) potatoes, diced
1 pint (600 ml) tinned tomatoes, chopped
1 pint (600 ml) water
1 tablespoon tomato purée
½ pint (300 ml) soured cream or thick Greek style yoghurt
Salt and pepper

Brown the mince and onion together in a saucepan. Add the herbs and spices and then the potatoes and cook for 1 minute. Add the remaining ingredients except the yoghurt and season with salt and pepper. Simmer until the potatoes are cooked, about 20 minutes. Serve piping hot with a spoon of yoghurt or soured cream on each bowl.

Quality mince

We have had several complaints from viewers about the quality of mince – too greasy, too fatty, bits of bone in it and generally not lean enough. 'What is the law?' they ask.

The law merely requires mince to be wholesome. But the shops are beginning to categorise it. The three categories of mince sold in supermarkets are

1 *Standard*, up to 25 per cent fat content

2 *Lean*, up to 18 per cent fat content

3 *Extra lean*, up to 10 per cent fat content

Prices currently range from £1.10 for the cheapest Standard to £2 for the most expensive Extra Lean.

The only way to be absolutely sure of the quality of mince is to ask your butcher to mince any cut for you, or mince your own in a food processor. If you feel you have bought mince that is badly sub-standard, report it to your local Trading Standards Office.

DELICIOUS LAMB

I'm very fond of lamb chops. They are quick, easy to cook and scrumptious – especially if I'm allowed to gnaw at the bony bits.

They have, however, as a nation diverted us from the virtues of the less neat and accessible cuts of lamb – breast and neck for instance. Here are a couple of my favourite dishes made from these extremely cheap and most tasty cuts. Don't worry about the combination of ingredients, they work wonderfully together.

MIDDLE EASTERN LAMB STEW
Serves 5 to 6

This recipe calls for cheaper cuts of lamb. Either scrag end of neck at 70p to £1.00 per lb (450 g) or middle neck chops at 90p to £1.70 per lb (450 g). Although these cuts are available at supermarkets, we found local butchers to be considerably cheaper. It is advisable to order these cuts in advance from your butcher, if using scrag end ask him to cut it into 1-in (2.5-cm) rounds.

For the lentils, you can use red or yellow lentils, or the slightly larger yellow Chana dal available from Indian supermarkets.

2 tablespoons olive oil
1½–2 lb (750g–2 kg) lamb
1 lb (450 g) onions, chopped
1 clove garlic, chopped
2 oz (50 g) red lentils
1 teaspoon ginger
1 teaspoon coriander
½ teaspoon cinnamon
A pinch of salt
4 oz (100 g) dried apricots
2 tablespoons browned, slivered almonds

Heat the oil in a large flameproof casserole, and brown the lamb. Add the onions, garlic and lentils and stir. Add the spices and salt and cook for 1 minute before adding enough water to just cover the lamb pieces. Add the apricots, cover the pan and cook for 1 hour on a low heat. The lentils and apricots will absorb the water and thicken the stew. Serve on a bed of pilau rice with spinach and sprinkle with the almonds.

PILAU RICE
Serves 6

Allow 2 oz (50 g) of rice per person and use twice the volume of water to rice. The best way of doing this is to measure out the amount of rice you will need and put it in a bowl or measure, you can then use this to measure two equal volumes of water.

12 oz (350 g) basmati rice
1 oz (25 g) butter
1 cinnamon stick
4 cardamon seeds
1 bay leaf
A few strands of saffron (this is one of the most expensive spices,
made from crocus stamens) or saffron powder
3 oz (75 g) raisins

Use a saucepan with a tightly fitting lid. Fry the rice in the butter to coat the grains. Add double the volume of water and the spices, bring to the boil, then turn down and cook for 15 minutes on a low heat. Put a tea towel over the pan when all the water is absorbed and leave for 5 minutes. Add the raisins and serve on an oval plate.

EPIGRAMS OF LAMB
Serves 4

An epigram is a brief witty joke. I hope these are appropriately named. They are not a joke but they are crisp, to the point and extremely diverting. They are also very good value.

1 breast of lamb
½ onion
1 bay leaf
1 egg, beaten
6 oz (175 g) soft fresh breadcrumbs

Trim excess fat off the meat, place in a saucepan and cover with water. Bring to the boil, drain and repeat, skimming off any froth, and adding the onion and bay leaf. Simmer for 50 minutes. Drain and cool, the bones should just pull away, discard them and the liquid. Cut the meat up into 1-in (2.5-cm) slices. Dip them in egg and then breadcrumbs, then grill under a hot grill for 3 to 5 minutes a side, until crisp and golden. Alternatively, you can pre-heat the oven to 400°F (200°C), gas mark 6, and bake them on a baking sheet for about 20 minutes. Serve with mashed potatoes and tartare sauce.

RABBIT RECIPES
Rabbit used to be a great luxury when it was first brought to Britain in medieval times. Then it became a despised pest and myxomatosis followed. Now it's available again and ready to be turned into

lovely rustic-flavoured dishes of some delicacy. (Fresh farm rabbit is delicious and good value, it has very little fat and tastes similar to chicken. If your butcher does not have any you can order it. Many supermarkets sell various cuts as well as frozen cubes. Wild rabbit is more difficult to get hold of, it can be tougher and richer and more gamey in taste.) Don't be put off by the Beatrix Potter image, she also wrote Jemima Puddleduck, and most of us enjoy Canard à l'Orange, don't we? Two traditional rabbit stews, then, one from our own countryside, and one with the compliments of Antonio Carluccio from the kitchens of a Tuscan castle.

MR McGREGOR'S RABBIT STEW
Serves 4

2 tablespoons oil
1 oz (25 g) butter
A little flour
1 rabbit, cut into large pieces
8 oz (225 g) onion, finely chopped
1 lb (450 g) leeks, cleaned and cut into 1-in (2.5-cm) pieces
1 lb (450 g) carrots, cut into 1-in (2.5-cm) pieces
8 oz (225 g) celery, cut into 1-in (2.5-cm) pieces
¾ pint (450 ml) good apple juice
2 bay leaves
Parsley stalks
Marjoram
Salt and pepper
6 small whole onions, peeled
1 tablespoon made mustard

Heat the oil and butter in a flameproof casserole. Lightly flour the pieces of rabbit and brown in the fat. When golden add the finely chopped onion and fry for a few minutes. Add the leeks, carrots and celery, stir well and fry for 5 minutes, then add the apple juice, bay leaves, parsley stalks, marjoram and season well. Place the whole onions on the top of the casserole, cover and cook gently for 1 hour either on top of the stove or in a moderate oven pre-heated to 325°F (160°C), gas mark 3. When it is cooked stir in the mustard and serve with Brussels sprouts and new potatoes.

SIGNOR CARLUCCIO'S RABBIT WITH ROSEMARY
Serves 6
This recipe for rabbit or chicken is simple and delicious.

3-4 lb (1.5-1.75 kg) rabbit, cut into good-sized pieces still on the bone
1 tablespoon salt
1 teaspoon black pepper
1 wine glass olive oil
5 fresh sprigs of rosemary, or 1 tablespoon of dried
1 glass white wine

Wash and dry the rabbit and coat with the salt and pepper. Heat the olive oil in a large heavy bottomed frying pan. Add the rabbit and rosemary and fry on a high heat until the rabbit is golden in colour. This will take about 10 minutes. Add the white wine and cook on a low heat so the juices just simmer for 40 to 50 minutes. Leave the pan uncovered during cooking even if you choose to cook the dish in an oven. Serve with fried potatoes and a fresh green salad.

ROAST BEEF

Before I indulge one of my favourite tastes – for offal, and liver in particular – many of the viewers of *Food and Drink* asked to have the Crafty Roast Beef recipe repeated. Here it is. It works well for all roasting joints, but I recommend the fore rib, often called the butcher's roast because no-one buys it and it is the experts' favourite. Rich flavoured, easy serving and about half the price of sirloin!

Pre-heat the oven to 425°F (220°C), gas mark 7. Place the meat on a wire rack, season with a little pepper and place on a roasting pan. Put the dish into the oven and immediately turn down the temperature to 350°F (180°C), gas mark 4. (The intense heat at the beginning seals the meat, preventing loss of juices and flavour. The lower temperature allows it to cook without burning.) Cook the joint for 12 to 15 minutes per pound (450 g), if you like your meat well done add a couple of minutes per pound. After 20 minutes, put 1 pint (600 ml) of water in the pan to make the gravy. Remove from the oven and leave to 'rest' for 5 minutes per pound. That can mean up to 30 minutes. It will make *all* the difference to carving and eating.

LIVER

'Offal isn't awful' is hardly a new slogan, yet we tend to regard it as a lower class of nourishment. The only exception would be calves' liver if its current price is anything to go by. Though it's delicious, so too is lambs' liver and chicken liver – at about a quarter to one sixth of the price. So although you can use calves' liver for my first two liver recipes, the crafty advice is try lambs'.

LIVER IN AN ORANGE GLAZED SAUCE
Serves 4

This recipe has a sweet/sour flavour. Use thinly sliced lambs' or calves' liver. Cut out any tubes and if you wish you can remove any skin along the edges of each slice. The following recipe will cook up to four pieces of liver depending on the size of your pan. The pieces should not overlap or they will not seal well. If you want to fry more pieces use two pans.

4 oz (100 g) plain flour
½ teaspoon paprika
½ teaspoon ground bay leaf
Salt and pepper
4 pieces liver, thinly sliced
2 tablespoons olive oil for frying
Worcestershire sauce
½ wine glass high juice orange squash

Mix the flour, paprika, bay leaf, salt and pepper together on a plate. Lightly coat the liver in the flour. Heat the oil until very hot in a frying pan and add the liver, cook for 20 to 30 seconds before turning the liver over. Add a shake of Worcestershire sauce and the orange squash, fry for another 20 to 30 seconds and serve with a little of the sauce. The liver should be just pink in the middle.

FEGATO VENEZIANO
Serves 4

The Italian style of liver and onions is quickly cooked and quite different from our own (see below). Make sure the liver slices are thin and flat. The closer they are in shape to a postcard the better for this dish.

2 tablespoons olive oil
1 lb (450 g) onions, thinly sliced
4 tablespoons white wine vinegar
1 lb (450 g) lambs' or calves' liver, thinly sliced
Salt and pepper

Heat the oil and fry the onions very gently until soft but *not* browned, about 10 to 15 minutes. Turn the heat up, add the vinegar, and when it boils, add the liver. Cook for only 30 seconds, turn and cook for 1 minute. Season and serve. The Venetians (where the recipe comes from) eat it with rice cooked with green peas.

LIVER AND ONION CASSEROLE
Serves 4

Ox liver, plenty of onions and thick gravy is the order of the day here, but don't be tempted to revert to the canteen method of flavouring using beef cubes. This dish has plenty of flavour of its own.

1½ lb (750 g) ox liver
6 tablespoons seasoned flour
4 tablespoons oil or beef dripping
1½ lb (750 g) onions, peeled and thickly sliced
1 tablespoon Worcestershire sauce
8 oz (225 g) carrots, peeled and sliced
Salt and pepper

Pre-heat the oven to 325°F (160°C), gas mark 3. Slice the liver into 1-in (2.5-cm) thick slices and coat in the flour. Heat the oil or dripping in a flameproof casserole and fry the liver steadily until well browned. Add the onions and the Worcestershire sauce and cook for 5 minutes. Add the carrots, season and add enough water to come just below the liver and onion mixture. Bring to the boil and then put in the oven for 1 hour. Serve with plenty of boiled or mashed potatoes and some crisp cabbage.

CHICKEN LIVER KEBABS
Serves 4

Incredibly cheap and easy to cook, these kebabs have ancestors from as far apart as Crete and Japan. One of the secrets is to use thin wooden or bamboo skewers, easily obtainable from kitchen shops or Chinese/South-East Asian style shops. They don't break up the chicken livers when they thread them, and the ends don't get hot.

1 clove garlic, peeled
½ teaspoon salt
4 tablespoons olive or salad oil
1 lemon
½ teaspoon ground cumin
1½ lb (750 g) chicken livers

Crush the garlic with the salt, and stir into the oil and the juice of the lemon with the cumin powder. Add the livers, cut in even-sized 1-in (2.5-cm) chunks and marinate 1 to 4 hours. Thread on to 8 skewers, keeping them close together at the sharp end. Grill under a hot grill for 2 minutes each side or until brown and bubbling. Serve with rice or in pitta bread, warmed in the oven and part-filled with salad.

QUALITY MEAT

There is a new movement amongst butchers to provide us with 'modern' cuts of meat – less fat, more convenience. I do hope it goes with animals kept in decent conditions and humanely slaughtered, not something I'm always sure of these days. I also hope that it goes with meat properly 'hung'; that is allowed to mature properly after slaughter, for the flavour and tenderness to develop. Do ask about this. It can be up to three weeks hanging for good beef and some carrying the Scotch Aberdeen Angus labels guarantee this.

New butchery

Amongst the new types of butchery recommended by the Meat and Livestock Commission are:

Continental cuts – cutting along the muscle enabling more fat to be trimmed off.
Lamb Valentine Steaks.
Lamb leg steaks.
Stir-fry beef.
'All-in-one' stewing beef (with carrots and leeks inserted into the meat).

You might be hard put to find it in supermarkets, whatever marketing labels they hang on – so find a good butcher. There is a new group of craftsmen promising butchering at a quality of service and produce that is to be applauded. They are called the 'Q' guild. If you are a butcher and would like to enquire about joining the 'Q' guild, or would like to know your nearest 'Q' guild butcher you can call Tim Green on this number: 0908 648564.

LOCAL FLAVOUR

REAL ALE
JILL GOOLDEN

The sight of a glass of wine conjures up pictures of a bosomy vine-yard slope bulging with juicy grapes awaiting the gnarled peasant hand to snip them off in their prime. But as for a glass of beer? The imagination has difficulty running beyond the bottle it was poured from, or perhaps a canning plant, or an unromantic steel keg. How sad that most of us now see our national drink, an ancient part of our heritage, as just another industrial product. For me, it took a visit to a 'home-brew pub' where you can see the 'baby' being born and nurtured before your eyes, to bring home the fact that beer can have its own peculiar pedigree and personality.

The nuances of difference between beers – and families of beers – have been somewhat smudged under the 'complex monopoly' that has existed in British pubs, nearly 50 per cent of which have been tied to one of six brewers (Allied, Bass, Courage, Grand Metropolitan, Scottish and Newcastle, and Whitbread) and bound to sell only their beers. According to CAMRA (the Campaign for Real Ale) even the majority of so called 'free' houses have been linked in some way to one of the big brewers – hence the recent investigation by the Monopolies and Mergers Commission and the renewed concern about the situation shown by the EEC Commission.

The MMC report last spring recommended a huge shake-up of the industry with the 'big brewers' being forced to loosen their grip at the consumer end. It was suggested that they should relinquish 22 000 pubs on to the open market where, it was hoped, they would fall into new hands and become free to sell any beers they chose – and at any price. The ideal would have been for these pubs to be bought either by small regional brewers, or by individuals wishing to set up a genuinely free house without obligations to any brewer.

But in an unprecedented self-funded advertising campaign, the brewers threatened simply to unload their remoter, less viable hostelries at present, they claimed, doing more to serve the local community than their masters' pockets. These pubs would then simply disappear forever, so the brewers warned, which would have a savage impact on the British way of life. Another unsung, and unwelcome, alternative would have been for the major brewers to let the requisite number of pubs go – probably to leisure conglomerates – and instead concentrate their mighty strength on being mega-brewers, offering such massive discounts to the new owners that no small brewer could possibly compete.

Already it's not unusual for incentives of £40 to £50 a barrel discount to be offered by the big boys – that is actually the total profit (maybe more) for a small brewer. If the big brewers had concentrated their might and monopoly in this way the result could have been even less competition and considerably fewer beers to choose from (as has already happened in Australia and the US).

The hold the big six brewers have on the market has always appeared to the sceptics to be sufficiently strong to block the introduction of any radical measures aimed at dismantling their monopoly, and indeed, the sceptics have been proved right. The Commission's radical plans have now been abandoned in the face of a lethally effective lobby by the brewers. In July, Lord Young announced that: brewers will not have to sell any pubs, but that those owning more than 2000 will have to keep half the additional pubs as genuinely free houses. Within that they can still set up further ties if they wish. The only exception is that the 'big six' will not be able to insist they supply wine, spirits and soft drinks. That small victory is accompanied by a promise to renew licensing systems which may at present (and we have evidence of this) prevent small brewers from running pubs. All in all, a big retreat from the original proposals, and what a pity.

Long before the Government saw fit to intercede, CAMRA, almost single handedly, fought long and hard for the revival of *real flavour* in our beers and the return of real choice. And they have achieved a great deal. But they have been battling against Goliath. Mass-produced beers dominate the arena, and are generally awash with adjuncts, additives and preservatives included in the recipe expressly to give that homogeneity those of us looking for Real Flavour deplore – and, of course, a necessarily long and stable life if they have far to travel to pubs in the brewery's chain all over the country.

There have always been small, independent brewers, of course, but they have had an extremely tough time finding outlets for their beers in an essentially closed market. Gaining a new licence, according to Paul Soden, Chairman of the Small Independent Brewers Association, has been 'more or less impossible'. During the last ten years, for the 144 courageous new small-scale breweries that have been set up, 143 have had to close.

Prior to the proposed shake-up, less than a pitiful 1 per cent of the industry was controlled by the small independent brewers. The Big Six brewers have 75 per cent of the market; eleven large regional breweries, 11 per cent; forty-one local brewers control 6 per cent; three large brewers with no pubs (including Guinness) have 8 per cent. So there you have 100 per cent; it's just the odd pip of shortfall that goes to make the 'under 1 per cent'.

The first 'home-brew pub' – that is a pub brewing its own beer on the premises – I ever visited was the Falcon and Firkin in Hackney, where the steamy brewing process takes place beside the main bar, visible through a large plate glass window. And it is a mesmerising sight. Gone are the mass-produced factory images; the glass of beer in your hand at this pub (and remarkable beer it is, too) paints pictures of steam and hops and wash-tuns, of dedication and hard work.

Once an industrial revolution has dawned, it's no use romanticising about the days when everything was done by hand, probably much less efficiently and taking twice as long. You might say that I'm getting close to this fantasy in waxing lyrical about the on-the-spot brewer and his pub. But hear me out! There is a lot of scope for beer, whether it be bitter, stout, porter, lager, mild or ale to be hand-crafted to an individual recipe, to have a unique character and style all of its own. And if you, like me, are interested in subtle differences in flavour, in quality for its own sake, it's worth having a sniff about your locality to find anyone making – or selling – individual hand-crafted beer. It would be magical if the eventual effect of the MMC report could be to increase the number of these idiosyncratic concerns and their beers.

Inspired by the joys of the Falcon and Firkin, I decided to seek out other micro breweries, and settled on the West Country for my delightful pub crawl. First stop, Penarth near Cardiff at what claims to be the smallest commercial brewery in Britain, the Raisdale Sparging and Brewing Company at Raisdale House Hotel. Patron and chief brewer is Steven Simpson-Wells who came to brewing by the rather unorthodox route of carpet laying, ski instructing and salvage diving. But brewing isn't simply another notch in his colourful belt, it is Steven's consuming passion.

And you could say he's not merely a brewer, but an inventor, having tuned the brewing process to suit his own very specific, and modest, needs. 'Producing in such small volume – just over a barrel a week, which is enough to keep the hotel guests happy – I found heating and cooling large quantities of water was uneconomical, so I invented a revolutionary process,' Steven explained. Revolutionary and secret, because Steven has plans to franchise his unique methods. As near as I got to finding out the secret was a glimpse into his garden shed, the brewing HQ, where there is a ten-gallon Burco boiler, plastic wine fermenters, plastic tubes and an elementary bottling line.

A wide range of bottle-conditioned beers is Steven's speciality; wonderful beers with marvellous names. Perhaps the most unusual is Lucifer Pilsner – a type of beer that is so rare it is virtually extinct: bottle-conditioned lager. Lager *means* to condition or keep, but get-rich-quick brewers aren't interested in keeping the stuff; it's not profitable, especially since the hefty duty levied on beer is payable at the making, rather than the selling stage in the chain. Conditioning the lager costs the brewer months of interest. You could say most British lagers contravene the Trade Descriptions Act in not being 'lagered' at all ... Raisdale's lager, though, is kept for about twelve weeks on the lees (the yeast and gubbins) in bottle, producing a powerfully flavoured, full bodied lager of 4 per cent alcohol. (Percentage alcohol by volume measures the strength of a drink. Most beers are 4 to 6 per cent by volume, wine averages 12 per cent.)

O'Hooligan's Revolt is another relative rarity, a bottle-conditioned stout as smooth, velvety and lush as you could possibly wish for. I'm a great fan of stout, and this version reaches echelons most other stouts can only aspire to. Looby's Lust, named after his wife, is an old ale; 8-Bore Special a draught bitter, and Stanley's Steamhammer a (bottle conditioned, of course) celebration ale to mark his daughter, Stanley's, birth (the steamhammer bit refers to her heartbeat).

Brewing for a residents' only hotel has been the first stepping stone in Steven's brewing career. Next step will be a pub if and when he can find a promising one to buy. 'I can't wait for the Monopolies report to take effect – I'm determined to get a pub this year come what may,' he told me at the time of the Commission's report. Let's hope he will not now be disappointed.

The Fleece and Firkin in Bristol was originally a David Bruce pub (he, the patron saint of small brewers, successfully reviving the home-brew pub) before being sold to Halls. Despite its inclusion in the massive Allied group, the Bruce spirit is maintained in this marvellous Georgian wool merchants' hall, where beer brewed on the premises by Karen Warburton is swilled down to live (positively hyperactive when I was there) music and entertainment (jelly wrestling, chandelier swinging, what you will).

Karen is a kind of learn-as-you-go brewer, sliding across from her barmaid post when the last brewer moved on. And she has kept up his list of cask beers, sticking faithfully to his methods – usually laudable, although adjuncts (slightly unorthodox ingredients used for reasons of economy or expedience) do creep in here and there.

Classically, all beer derives from four basic ingredients: malted barley, yeast, hops and water. That sounds simple enough, but determining the right proportions and transforming these ingredients into a unique brew is an art. Beer expert Michael Jackson considers beer a much more complicated drink to make than wine, with more variables than you could possibly dream of. All professional brewers are capable of brewing a good pint, though it is widely acknowledged that many compromise perfection for profits – and in the case of the big boys, for homogeneity, too. So if you learn your skills in the 'compromise' school, you learn – wittingly or unwittingly – to compromise.

Funnily enough, Karen's brews have the stamp of the female brewer about them. I was cruel enough to liken her ordinary bitter to the only (extremely amateurish) attempt I made at this brewing lark; it somehow lacks courage. Stronger ales are her forte, with her Cole Porter hitting the spot admirably with a lovely dark, nutty twang to it. Porter was originally a London style – a kind of lighter bodied stout, but it was seen off by mild and became extinct. Happily a porter revolution is going on; it's good stuff and shouldn't be allowed to die out.

As my pub crawl developed, so did my thirst, and battling my way to the bar in the Jolly Roger in Worcester I knew exactly why the throngs of locals were crowded in the smoky, noisy bar. They were there for the beer. Paul Soden, landlord and brewer of the Jolly Brewer home-brew pub is a fanatic, determined to make the best beer in the world. His first brewery experiment began in his bedroom at sixteen. He now owns and brews for two pubs, and designs and sells brewing equipment, acting as a consultant to newcomers to his trade. One of his more recent consultancy customers was a Frenchman in Rouen, now making 'fizzy lager' for his bar from English ale vats installed by Paul.

To get round the licensing restrictions, Paul sold his first commercial pints at his private 'club', which emulates (give or take the odd juke box) a medieval pub with the brewery beside the bar. And two years ago the club was granted a full licence and the Jolly Roger brewery took over a smarter hostelry across the road as well. His weakest pint is Quaff Bitter, at less than 4 per cent alcohol – a fruity, light, hoppy glassful; Old Lowesmoor is a strong English ale at 5.5 to 6 per cent that is so substantial and full bodied it seems 'fat'. Winter Wobbler is brewed to keep out the cold, among other things, at 11 per cent or so, and annually Paul organises the Wobbler run to Rouen . . . on Beaujolais Nouveau day.

Although delighted, on behalf of the small brewers, that the 'scandalous' activities of the big brewers have been exposed by the Monopolies report, he was always sceptical about the eventual benefits to the likes of himself. Had *he* been in charge, he would have made two very specific recommendations: namely that a sliding scale of duty should be introduced, meaning the smaller the brewer, the less he pays (this operates widely in Continental Europe, encouraging thousands of small breweries on to the market, and seems like an excellent and simple way of controlling the major brewers' market dominance). He would also have obliged all bars to offer two guest beers – with (vital this, he thinks) adequate provision made for policing the system to make sure no 'fixing' goes on behind the scenes. As it now stands, pubs owned by national breweries must offer one guest beer (the regional brewers being exempt). No plans for policing the system have been announced.

Paul Soden is well prepared for any relaxation of the stranglehold; he is planning a showcase brewery with an output of a hundred barrels a week. He was also ready to snap up a few more pubs had they been forced to be sold. . . . He may well be disappointed there.

The Burton Bridge brewery sitting plonk in the middle of Burton-on-Trent, home of the British brewing tradition and two of the Big Six, is one of the largest small independents, making forty to fifty barrels of delicious nectar a week. They have only one pub, beside the brewery in Burton, and so as one of the directors, Geoff Mumford, said when Lord Young first made his recommendation, 'looking on the bright side, according to the report we've got 1999 to go' . . .

He left his cushy job with one of the largest brewery companies, Ind Coope, and joined forces with Bruce Wilkinson, a former Ind Coope brewer, to set up the Burton Bridge brewery in a delightful, dilapidated old brewery in this famous brewing town (with 'perfect water'). They wanted to be in business on their own and they wanted to make 'great beer'. Essentially Bruce makes it and Geoff sells it to pubs around the country – the number of pubs they deliver to on an irregular basis has risen to 400 since I visited them on my pub crawl, and they have had to buy a larger lorry (with a tail lift, I'm glad to say – on my visit they had me loading the pins by hand as drayman's assistant).

It's hard work making beer, as I discovered. I was tricked by Bruce into one of the toughest manual jobs – digging out the mash tun. He told me that if I completed the arduous (and hot and steamy) task, I could 'stand up at a brewery dinner'. Sounded like a rather curious honour to me, but I took to the challenge. It wasn't until I'd finished that he let on that brewery dinners are men only affairs . . .

Anyway. I'd earned my pint. Geoff served me in the bar next door. 'Something quite weak,' I said feebly, 'I'm dying of thirst.' 'You don't want a fortnight one do you?' 'What's that?' I asked. 'Too weak!' Burton Bridge doesn't sell fortnight ones, though, I discovered. I opted for Bridge Bitter, wonderful stuff (and thirst quenching) with complex malty, hoppy flavours. Burton Festival – sweeter and stronger – was tailor-made for a beer festival and has remained in the repertoire. Their bottle-conditioned porter, dark and bitter, is wonderful – and has even earned a fan club on the other side of the Atlantic.

The Monopolies and Mergers Commission investigation was initiated in part to see if small companies such as Burton Bridge are getting a fair crack. And its findings clearly show that they are not. But can they expect a better deal in the future? Geoff stops his wise-cracking for a moment and admits he and Bruce have a 'dismal view' of the final outcome. Rather than better, they think things could become considerably worse.

'The major brewers have been at it for so long ['it' being tying up the market to their own advantage] they're not going to stand back and simply allow their guts to be ripped out. They'll fight and so much dust will be kicked up into the atmosphere that they'll be able to slip and slide through, probably into a more powerful position than before.' His predictions are proving all too right.

Although Geoff boasted of 'another 1999 pubs to go', they can't actually afford to buy a second one; they have chosen to concentrate on brewing instead. But unless the Government's intervention is effective, it's possible they, too, could go under, to round the casualty figures for small brewers up to a full gross.

Real ale

The four brewing companies visited by Jilly were:

Burton Bridge Brewery,
Bridge Street,
Burton-on-Trent,
Staffordshire.
Telephone: 0283 510573 for the names of other pubs serving their beer.

Fleece and Firkin,
12 St Thomas Street,
Bristol,
Avon.

Jolly Roger Brewery and Tap,
50 Lowesmoor,
Worcester,
Hereford and Worcester.

Raisdale Sparging and Brewing Co.,
Raisdale House,
Raisdale Road,
Penarth,
South Glamorgan.

Two publications list small brewers and home-brew pubs:

Camra New Beer Guide by Brian Glover (David and Charles £3.95).

Camra 1989 Good Beer Guide (Camra £5.95)

Both books are available by post from
Camra Ltd,
34 Alma Road,
St Albans,
Hertfordshire AL1 3BW
Telephone: 0727 67201.

THE PUDDING CLUB

INTRODUCTION
CHRIS KELLY

The desire to eat healthily and stay slim, though laudable in many ways, has all but buried a great British treasure. Dig back into our culinary heritage and you'll find we were once world leaders in puddings. We were, in fact, 'the puddin'-race' par excellence. Before the War, kitchens across the nation regularly steamed with glorious afters. A few of these substantial treats even survived into the fifties and sixties. Now, however, they're about as fashionable as antimacassars.

Just to recite the litany of our lost desserts is both to realise what we're missing and to indulge in potent nostalgia: the classic spotted dick, forever reminiscent of dubbined football boots, ink-stained fingers and chilblains; jam roly-poly, with its Pickwickian echoes of rosy warmth and well-being; Sussex pond pudding, a witness to the days before concrete jungles.

In resisting sweet temptation we have of course over-reacted. The reality is that, as part of a balanced diet, the occasional pudding is absolutely fine. Better still, if it makes us feel good, it's something to be welcomed and encouraged.

Having swallowed our absurd guilt, however, we're liable to face a further problem, at least when we're eating out. The choice of desserts on offer in most British restaurants is the gastronomic equivalent of Esperanto. Far from reflecting our native tradition, it more or less ignores home-grown puds. Profiteroles abound, along with sticky gateaux, but where is the ginger sponge? Most peculiar of all is the case of the ubiquitous crème brulée. Unquestionably English in origin (burnt cream), and ancient at that, it has somehow been credited to the French.

Confronted with this sad decline, we were immensely heartened when news reached the *Food and Drink* office of a rearguard action. Here's how the story unfolded. In 1983, Keith and Jean Turner, who had farmed a smallholding in the Lake District for seven years on 'good life' principles, were asked by friends to share management of a Cotswolds hotel, The Three Ways at Mickleton. One day, shortly after moving in, they were mourning the passing of the pudding in a Malvern pub. Why not revive it, they thought aloud, by forming a pudding club, dedicated to its preservation? Earwigging, a total stranger beside them at the bar almost fell off his stool in his eagerness to join.

Two weeks later the inaugural meeting was held at The Three Ways. Keith, a former management consultant, went to town with a brochure strong on whimsy. Twenty devotees turned up, and a delightfully eccentric institution was born. Today, demand for places at pudding club evenings far outstrips supply.

When I drove over to investigate the phenomenon, the first thing that struck me was a great wave of warmth and hospitality. Jean Turner, for many years a dental surgeon, believes running a hotel can be a sort of healing process. Guests who leave relaxed and at ease with themselves, she reasons, will be better able to cope with subsequent pressures. What a rare approach, and how refreshing. Other managements please note. The philosophy is infectious. The entire staff appeared motivated and genuinely pleased to be of service.

Guests, fifty-nine of them, began to arrive about seven o'clock and proved a friendly, polyglot crowd. Word of the fabulous puddings had clearly spread far beyond these shores. I met visitors from Germany, the United States, Venezuela, Canada and Japan. Over a glass of gooseberry wine they chatted animatedly, fired with anticipation by friends who had been before. Keith Turner, life president of the pudding club, then announced the rules with the mock gravity of Old Tyme Music Hall. No starters, to leave more room for the crowning glory; or rather seven crowning glories, which would follow the main course. As each of the puddings was announced, the diners gasped and cheered: queen of puddings; spotted dick; preserved ginger pudding; Lord Randall's pudding (suggested by a member); Mrs Beeton's chocolate pud, with a velvety chocolate sauce; coffee and walnut fudge pudding, swimming in butterscotch; and blackberry Exeter pudding. At the end of the evening a vote would be taken to decide the winner. We were encouraged to eat as many puddings as we liked, and more than one helping of each would entitle us to more than one vote.

Excitement peaked when, an hour or so later, the contenders were carried in solemn parade from the kitchen to the serving table. Beside this, Miss World was a non-event. Connoisseurs compared vital statistics. Eyes shone with recognition and roars greeted old favourites. Up we trooped for pud after irresistible pud. A Venezuelan at my table managed nine helpings and had to be nursed through a spell of breathlessness. I have never seen a more contented patient.

Debate raged. Finally Keith called us to order and we reviewed the candidates. If only General Elections were this much fun. Enthusiasts lobbied shamelessly for their nominees and the odds seemed finely balanced. At the count, however, one name outpolled all others, brilliantly routing the opposition. The undisputed champion of champions was Lord Randall's Pudding (see below), flavoured with thick marmalade and dried apricots; a delicious alternative to Christmas pudding.

If you seek proof that British puddings are alive and well after all, and if you enjoy good company in a jolly atmosphere, the pudding club is a must. A word of warning, however. Since our film, The Three Ways has had more than 800 letters of enquiry, some including recipes. There are unlikely to be many spare places before the spring of 1990. There has even been a tentative invitation for Keith and Jean to put on an evening of British puddings in Paris. How satisfying that would be. Perhaps we can reintroduce the French to authentic burnt cream?

Meanwhile, why not set up a pudding club in your area? You

The pudding club

You can contact the experts at:

The Three Ways Hotel,
Mickleton,
Near Chipping Campden,
Gloucestershire GL55 6SB
Telephone: 0386 438429.

The pudding club season runs from September until April. From autumn 1989, the price of a ticket will be £12 (including a pre-dinner glass of wine).

---

can use the recipes in this chapter as a starting point. It's easy to organise and I guarantee you'll be overwhelmed by the response. All of which seems to suggest that, like King Arthur, the taste for our native puds has not been dead at all but merely sleeping. We owe it to ourselves to bring about their renaissance.

RECIPES
MICHAEL BARRY

Puddings and the British – the most amazingly inseparable companions. Three dishes it seems to me, we have a reaction to that is almost beyond conscious control: roast lunch on Sundays; pies, not tarts; and puddings. Puddings of all kinds – steamed, Christmas, jam, ginger. The Pudding Club is just the elegant and scrumptious tip of the iced berg. So here are their seven best with ten of my own with a slightly lighter touch for those occasions when you need a lift not an anchor. The number refers to the puddings' placing in the club tasting Chris Kelly attended.

1ST – LORD RANDALL'S PUDDING
Serves 6

This is a deliciously light steamed pudding due to the relatively small amount of flour. As a result it does not turn out from the pudding basin in a firm shape, but the taste more than makes up for this.

4 oz (100 g) brown sugar
8 oz (225 g) butter
6 oz (175 g) dried apricots that have been soaked and chopped
8 oz (225 g) thick dark marmalade
4 oz (100 g) plain flour
1 egg + enough milk to make up 8 fl oz (250 ml)
1 teaspoon bicarbonate of soda
A pinch of salt

Cream the sugar and butter together until light and fluffy, then mix in the flour, bicarbonate of soda and salt. Mix well before adding the chopped apricots and marmalade. Gradually mix in the beaten egg and milk. Pour into a greased pudding basin, cover with greaseproof paper tied with string, and pleated kitchen foil. Steam for 3 hours. Check the steaming water occasionally to prevent the pan boiling dry.

2ND – SPOTTED DICK
Serves 4

8 oz (225 g) self-raising flour
A pinch of salt
4 oz (100 g) shredded suet
1 oz (25 g) sugar
8 oz (225 g) currants or raisins
¼ pint (150 ml) cold water

Stir together the flour, salt, suet, sugar and dried fruit. Mix to a firm dough with water. Form into a cylinder about 8 in (20 cm) long and put on a pudding cloth that has been wrung out in hot water and sprinkled with flour. Roll the pudding in the cloth and tie the ends tightly but leave room for expansion. Put into a pan of boiling water, cover and boil for 2 hours, adding more boiling water if necesary to prevent boiling dry. Turn the pudding on to a hot dish and serve with custard.

3RD – BLACKBERRY EXETER PUDDING
Serves 4

1½ lb (750 g) suet crust pastry
1 lb (450 g) breadcrumbs
4 oz (100 g) shredded suet
8 oz (225 g) runny honey
1 lb (450 g) apples
1 lb (450 g) blackberries

Line a greased pudding basin with two-thirds of the suet pastry and reserve the rest for the lid. Mix together the breadcrumbs, shredded suet, and honey until combined. Place half the apples and blackberries in the bottom of the basin, cover with a layer of honey-crumb mix and repeat. Place on the lid (you may need to wet the edges of the pastry with water to make it stick), cover with greaseproof paper and pleated kitchen foil and steam for 2 to 3 hours. Check the steaming water occasionally to prevent the pan boiling dry.

BUTTERSCOTCH SAUCE
Serves 4

6 oz (175 g) butter
3 tablespoons golden syrup
1 lb (450 g) demerara sugar
15 oz (425 g) evaporated milk

Melt the butter, add the syrup and sugar, and stir until the sugar has dissolved and all the ingredients are blended together. Pour in the evaporated milk, turn up the heat and beat until boiling.

DATE AND LEMON PUDDING
Serves 4

For the pudding:
3 oz (75 g) plain flour
½ teaspoon salt
1 teaspoon baking powder
½ oz (15 g) sugar
3 oz (75 g) shredded suet
3 oz (75 g) white breadcrumbs
3 oz (75 g) dates, chopped
10 oz (275 g) mixed dried fruit
Grated rind and juice of 1 lemon
1 egg
6 tablespoons fresh milk

For the sauce:
½ oz (15 g) cornflour
½ oz (15 g) custard powder
1 oz (25 g) sugar
¾ pint (450 ml) fresh milk
Grated rind and juice of 1 lemon
1 oz (25 g) butter

Sieve the flour, salt and baking powder into large bowl. Stir in the remaining ingredients and mix well. Pour into a buttered 1½-pint (1-l) pudding basin, cover with greaseproof paper and foil. Secure using string. Steam for 2 hours, checking the water occasionally. Make the sauce as for real egg custard and add the rind, juice and butter after it has thickened.

PINEAPPLE AND COCONUT PUD
Serves 8

This pudding has a shortcake base and a delicious soft centred macaroon-type topping.

For the base:

8 oz (225 g) plain flour
4 oz (100 g) brown sugar
6 oz (170 g) butter

For the mixture:

4 eggs
8 oz (225 g) caster sugar
2 oz (50 g) plain flour
½ teaspoon baking powder
½ teaspoon salt
½ teaspoon cinnamon
8 oz (225 g) pineapple pieces, tinned or fresh
4 oz (100 g) desiccated coconut
2 oz (50 g) chopped mixed nuts
1 teaspoon vanilla essence
4 oz (100 g) glacé cherries

Pre-heat the oven to 350°F (180°C), gas mark 4. To make the base, mix the flour and sugar and rub in the butter. Press into the bottom of an 8- or 9-in (20- or 23-cm) spring-form cake tin. Bake for 20 minutes. Turn down the oven to 300°F (150°C), gas mark 2. Beat the eggs in a large bowl and add the caster sugar; whisk until thick, pale and light. Placing the bowl over a saucepan of simmering water will quicken the process. (If using an electric mixer no heat is required.) When thick, remove from the heat and whisk until cool. Lightly fold in the flour, baking powder, salt and cinnamon. Drain the pineapple pieces and add to the mixture with the coconut, nuts and vanilla and mix well. Lay the cherries on top of the base, cover with the mixture and bake for 1 hour 15 minutes.

This pudding is good hot or cold, and can be re-heated in a moderate oven. Serve with custard or vanilla ice-cream.

BREAD AND BUTTER PUDDING
Serves 4 to 6

10-12 slices white bread
4-6 oz (100-175 g) softened butter
Juice and rind of 1 orange
4 oz (100 g) sultanas, soaked in rum or brandy
3 eggs
1 pint (600 ml) milk
3 oz (75 g) caster sugar
Cinnamon or nutmeg

Pre-heat the oven to 400°F (200°C), gas mark 6. Grease a baking dish. Remove the crusts, and butter the bread. Line the bottom and sides of the dish with bread, and sprinkle with the orange juice and rind. Add half the sultanas. Add more bread and sultanas. Beat the eggs well, add the milk and sugar, and pour the mixture over the bread. Sprinkle with cinnamon or nutmeg. Bake for 30 minutes or until set.

STICKY TOFFEE PUDDING
Serves 12

4 oz (100 g) softened butter
12 oz (350 g) granulated sugar
1 lb (450 g) plain flour
2 teaspoons baking powder
2 eggs
12 oz (350 g) stoned dates
1 pint (600 ml) boiling water
2 teaspoons bicarbonate of soda
2 teaspoons vanilla essence

Pre-heat the oven to 350°F (180°C), gas mark 4. Cream the butter and sugar. Sieve the flour and baking powder. Beat the eggs into the butter and sugar. Add a little flour and continue beating for 1 minute. Mix in the rest of the flour. Flour the dates lightly and chop. Pour the boiling water over them. Mix in the bicarbonate of soda and vanilla. Add this to the cake mix and blend well together. Turn into a buttered 11 × 7-in (28 × 18-cm) cake tin or similar container. Bake for 1 hour or until a skewer inserted in the centre comes out clean. If browning too quickly, cover in foil.

RHUBARB FOOL
Serves 4

Rhubarb is a kind of joke to many of us – the shape – the name – even the teeth-furrying qualities of unripe rhubarb seem to evoke mirth. It's a pity because it's diverted us from the delicious quality of this vegetable-come-fruit. In Yorkshire, of course, where many things are different, it is taken most seriously. Specially forced rhubarb, the pale pink kind, is best for this recipe, both for the lovely colour and delicate flavour. Even this delicacy isn't at all expensive so make the most of its short season.

1 lb (450 g) forced rhubarb
4 oz (100 g) granulated sugar
8 oz (225 g) low fat fromage frais
4 oz (100 g) set yoghurt
2 tablespoons roughly chopped stem ginger (preserved)

Wash the rhubarb and cut the stalks into 1-in (2.5-cm) pieces. Put in a saucepan with the sugar and cook gently until the rhubarb is soft. Leave to cool and in the meantime beat the fromage frais and yoghurt together in a bowl. Whizz the rhubarb in a blender or food processor until smooth, add the stem ginger and whizz for a few seconds more; the ginger should be in small pieces. Fold the rhubarb into the yoghurt, creating a pretty rippled effect. Spoon into bowls or glasses and chill for at least 1 hour before serving.

JUNKETS
Serves 4

Junkets are a very old tradition in Britain, though there seems a fair chance that the French brought them over with the Bastard Duke William. The name comes from the rush basket colanders the dish used to be drained in, in Normandy. Try it now for a delicate and refreshing taste. You can make it with semi-skimmed milk if you want an even lighter version. Flavourings can be anything from the traditional tablespoon of brandy to (what I prefer) lemon or raspberry juice or vanilla essence – only one teaspoon. In Devon they top this with clotted cream and toasted almonds. It makes a very rich treat.

1 pint (600 ml) of milk
2 tablespoons sugar
1 teaspoon rennet
½ teaspoon nutmeg powder

Optional flavourings:
1 teaspoon vanilla essence or 1 tablespoon lemon or raspberry juice

Heat the milk until it is hot but you can still dip a finger in it without screaming (be careful). Dissolve the sugar and add the rennet and the flavourings. Put in a pretty basin and leave to set *out* of the fridge for 4 hours. Then chill for an hour and top if you fancy it.

AMERICAN APPLE PIE
Serves 4 to 6

This is my crafty version of the pie that mommy used to make: thick, rich and yet simple and unsophisticated. Very different in shape, texture and taste from modern British pies, it is actually a direct descendent of the baking our ancestors took across the 'pond' a couple of centuries ago. The colonists when they arrived were 3000 or more miles from any sources of food, and winters were often desperately short on supplies in the early years. There are records of them surviving on apple pies made from dried apples and the last of their flour. This version, while very nourishing, has a little more to offer than just survival.

For the pastry:
1 lb (450 g) plain flour
A pinch of salt
1 oz (25 g) sugar
4 oz (100 g) solid cooking fat (e.g. Trex)
4 oz (100 g) butter
A little cold water
A beaten egg or milk to glaze

For the pie filling:
2 oz (50 g) granulated sugar
2 tablespoons cornflour
1½ teaspoons cinnamon
A few cloves (optional)
2½ lb (1.25 kg) Bramley apples, peeled, cored and cut into small chunks
1 × 10 oz (275 g) tin of condensed milk
Beaten egg or milk to glaze

Pre-heat the oven to 400°F (200°C), gas mark 6. Line an 8- or 9-in (20- or 23-cm) deep pie dish or spring-form cake tin with two-thirds of the pastry. Mix the sugar, cornflour and spice into the apples and put in the pie. Pour on the condensed milk. Roll out the pastry lid, and seal the edges of the pie well. Decorate the pie with pastry cut outs, slit and glaze with a beaten egg or some milk. Bake in the hot oven for 40 minutes. This pie is best served warm.

FRENCH APPLE PUDDING
Serves 4

This is a pudding unlike any other I know – a kind of super-thick apple pancake that cooks so easily it always amazes me how little trouble it takes.

1 lb (450 g) cooking apples, peeled and cored
2 oz (50 g) butter
1 teaspoon ground cinnamon
2 oz (50 g) caster sugar
7 fl oz (200 ml) milk
2 eggs, beaten
2 teaspoons vanilla essence
4 tablespoons icing sugar
3 oz (75 g) flour
A pinch of salt

Pre-heat the oven to 350°F (180°C), gas mark 4. Slice the apples and cook in the butter for 3 minutes. Add the cinnamon and sugar. Blend the milk, eggs and vanilla essence until smooth and add the icing sugar, a little at a time, whisking as you go. Then add the flour and salt in the same way. Pour into a greased baking tray or china flan dish, add the apples and bake for 1¼ hours. Sprinkle sugar over and serve with lots of cream.

QUEEN'S PUDDING
Serves 4 to 6

This most unusual pudding, a variation of the baked Queen of Puddings, is made in a frying pan and is good hot or cold. It is very rich but not cloying. A good end to a meal of sharp flavours and strong tastes.

½ pint (300 ml) single cream
2 eggs
2 egg yolks
2 oz (50 g) caster sugar
½ teaspoon almond essence
2 oz (50 g) ground almonds
2 oz (50 g) fresh white breadcrumbs
1 oz (25 g) butter
Slivered almonds and glacé cherries to decorate

Bring the cream to a boil and set aside. Beat the eggs, yolks, sugar and essence together until doubled in bulk. Add the cream steadily and whisk until smooth. Fold in the almonds and breadcrumbs with a metal spoon. Melt the butter in a deep frying pan and cook the mixture until it thickens and sets, 4 to 5 minutes. Invert the pan and turn on to a serving plate; decorate with almonds and glacé cherries.

BERRY CREAM SPONGE
Serves 4 to 6

When strawberries are in season this makes a lovely easy pudding, but actually I think it's best with raspberries or blackberries. The slightly darker fruit with a sharper taste contrasts beautifully with the crisp, golden, sweet sponge and the lusciousness of the cream.

6 oz (175 g) caster sugar
6 oz (175 g) soft tub margarine
3 eggs, beaten
6 oz (175 g) self-raising flour
1 teaspoon vanilla essence
½ pint (300 ml) double cream
2 tablespoons sugar
8 oz (225 g) strawberries, raspberries or blackberries

Pre-heat the oven to 375°F (190°C), gas mark 5. Cream the sugar and margarine together until light and fluffy. Beat in the eggs, one at a time. Fold in the flour and vanilla essence. Pour into 2 × 7-in (18-cm) greased sandwich tins (or use non-stick ones). Bake for 25 minutes until risen and golden. Turn out and allow to cool on a wire rack. Beat the cream until thick, sweeten to taste (depending on berries used) with not more than 2 tablespoons of sugar. Spread half the cream on one cake, slice half the berries and lay them on top. Place the second cake on top, smooth side upwards. Spread the rest of the cream on top and decorate with the remaining berries.

The cake will keep for up to 2 hours in the fridge; after that the cream will start to collapse, so don't assemble it too soon.

WALNUT TREACLE TART
Serves 4 to 6

This is an adaptation of a traditional English recipe. The walnuts in it add a little crunch. It can be served warm or cold, but my preference is for warm, with a lot of pouring cream to go with it. About a million calories an ounce, and worth every one of them.

8 oz (225 g) shortcrust pastry (home-made or packet)
4 oz (100 g) butter
2 oz (50 g) sugar
2 eggs, beaten
6oz (175 g) golden syrup
4 oz (100 g) walnuts, finely chopped
Grated rind of 1 lemon
Juice of ½ lemon
A pinch of salt

Pre-heat the oven to 400°F (200°C), gas mark 6. Use the pastry to line an 8½-in (21.5-cm) tin with straight sides. Fill it with some kitchen foil to stop it bubbling in the middle, and bake it in the oven for about 10 minutes. Mix together the butter and sugar until they are smooth and beat in the eggs and syrup (warming it in a saucepan if it's too cold to pour). Add the walnuts, the grated rind and juice of the lemon and the salt. Turn the mixture into the pastry case, having first removed the kitchen foil. Bake at 350°F (180°C), gas mark 4 for 45 to 55 minutes, until the top is brown, crispy and scented. Try and let it cool enough not to burn your mouth! In fact, it tastes better eaten warm or cold.

CHRISTMAS PYRAMID
Serves 4

You can kill two birds with one stone with this amazing dessert. It doubles as an impressive centrepiece for the table. Also, after possibly overdoing the main course, you can help yourself when you like. Don't be afraid to decorate it flamboyantly – Christmas baubles, ribbon, even cake candles on the top – although don't forget to remove them before you tuck in. And, if you're short on time or effort, you can buy the meringues, although home-made ones will keep in an air-tight container for up to a week.

8 egg whites
1 lb (450 g) caster sugar

For the filling:
1 pint (600 ml) double cream or
¾ pint (450 ml) double cream and ¼ pint (150 ml) yoghurt
1 tablespoon instant coffee (or to taste)
2 tablespoons boiling water

Pre-heat the oven to 225°F (110°C), gas mark ¼. Whisk the egg whites until stiff, then gradually whisk in half the sugar and fold in the remainder. Pipe or place dessertspoonfuls of the mixture on to lightly greased greaseproof paper on a baking tray and bake for 1½ to 2 hours or until the meringues have dried out. Carefully remove from the paper and leave until cold. To make the filling, whisk the cream until thick. If using cream and yoghurt, whisk the cream first and then mix with the yoghurt. Dissolve the coffee in boiling water. Leave until cool and then mix into the cream. Sandwich pairs of meringues with a dessertspoon of filling and pile on a dish in a pyramid. Decorate.

Cream liqueur

This cream liqueur suggested by Jill and Oz Clarke for Christmas is cheaper to make than the commercial varieties are to buy . . . and it's equally wicked!

Cream liqueur - makes 6 small glasses

The sugar in this recipe should be infused with a vanilla pod for extra flavour. It takes 2 weeks for the vanilla flavour to seep into the sugar. You can use vanilla essence instead; add a few drops to the drink with the cream.

1 tablespoon soft brown vanilla sugar
2 tablespoons water
4 fl oz (120 ml) Drambuie
9 fl oz (275 ml) single cream
Ice

Boil the sugar and water until syrupy. Pour the Drambuie and cream into a cocktail shaker or jam jar over ice. Add the vanilla essence if using, then the sugar syrup. Shake and serve.

The Drambuie is also excellent as a base for Irish Coffee – simply add a measure to coffee and slowly pour double cream on top over the back of a spoon. The secret to success is not to let the spoon break the surface of the coffee.

MELONS

Melons are too often taken for granted as a pudding – they come in great variety and cut in clever shapes they delight the eye as well as refresh the palate. You can add a sprinkle of powdered ginger, or crushed ginger in syrup or salt to any melon to bring out its flavour.

Melon varieties

Many varieties of melon are now imported from around the world at various times of the year. Sweetness depends on ripeness – if the melon is soft at its top when pressed lightly between thumb and forefinger it is ripe. This may take a few days from the time of purchase.

Yellow Honeydew
A crisp sweet melon. It has a yellow skin and a white flesh. One of the cheaper varieties. Available from March to December, best in May and June.

White Honeydew
Less sweet than the yellow, with a more complex taste. It has a pale creamy skin and white flesh. Available from March to December but more difficult to find.

Galia
A chewy, intensely sweet melon. It is round, has a green mottled skin and green flesh. Available from March to December, best in May, June and July.

Cantaloupe
Very sweet and juicy and the most highly flavoured – almost aromatic. It is round with a buff coloured skin and apricot coloured flesh. Available from June to October, best in July.

Charantais
Very much like the galia, has a stripy, green skin and orangey-yellow sweet flesh. Available from June to October, best in June, July and August.

Watermelons
A very different melon, larger than others, with a shiny dark green skin. The flesh is bright pink, sweet and refreshing – rather like a sorbet. Unlike other melons the pips are an integral part of flesh. Available from March to December, best in June and July.

To cut a melon decoratively take a sharp pointed knife about 3 to 5 in (7.5 to 13 cm) long. Put the melon on a safe surface and push the knife in, point first, in a series of linked diagonal cuts thus:

Don't worry if you over-cut slightly. Go all the way around the equator of the melon. When the last and first cuts link up you will be able to separate the halves, now attractively decorated, and scoop out the seeds.

A LOAD OF APPLES AND PEARS

APPLE AND PEAR DRINKS
JILL GOOLDEN

Our heritage didn't get much of a look-in in the 1960s and early 1970s, when the fashion was for *now*. The 'me' generation was obsessed by the present and the future, and didn't have much time to spend looking over their shoulders at the past. Historic customs and traditions went out of the window, and things pastoral were considered to be only for the hicks down on the farm.

But the reliable old wheel of fashion has turned full circle now and here we all are with flowers on our frocks, country magazines on our knees, sitting in our rustic pine kitchens surrounded by baskets of healthy fresh fruit and vegetables . . . Nostalgia has become the buzzy new fad and our heritage is back. Among the success stories of the reminiscent 1980s you find cider, almost forgotten in the frenetic 'modern' period, but revived with a vengeance once pastoral orchards and things natural came back into vogue. Apple juice, too, has roared strongly into fashion, and to a lesser extent apple wine and alcoholic derivatives of the pear.

Cider deserves its resurgence – made traditionally from English-grown apples, it is a splendid drink. (And, incidentally, responds better than any other alcoholic drink I know to being dealcoholised.) But far more spectacular is the rise to fame of the fresh-pressed juice of the English apple. Where the fruit juice market has doubled over the past five years, our appetite for fresh pressed English apple juice has increased ten-fold, with getting on for a hundred different juices now available.

And I have to say rather presumptiously, I think *Food and Drink* has played its part in the apple juice revolution, five years ago exposing the huge chasm of difference in quality between apple juices made from concentrates imported from abroad and the fresh pressed juice of our own English fruit. There is no comparison; fresh pressed juice can be real nectar, encapsulating the delicious and very varied scents and flavours of the British orchard.

We undoubtedly produce some of the best apples in the world in Britain, with the flavour of the fruit concentrated magnificently over a slow, cool growing period. Historically the 'eaters' (as opposed to the cookers or cider apples) were produced largely for the table. The major supermarkets, though, became so idealistic, demanding such consistently high cosmetic standards of uniformity and perfection that much fruit – if it had a blemish or was too large or too small – went to waste. The fresh-pressed juice fad has in fact come to the rescue of many despairing fruit farmers and we're all benefitting.

As a public and private fan of English apple juice, last year I was delighted to be a judge of the British Apple Juice Competition at the Marden Fruit Show (considered to be the premier apple show in Europe), along with Willy Rushton and Dr Owen Tucknott, a food flavour chemist. And again I was reminded just how astonishingly varied apple juices can be – almost vying with wine in their range of scents and flavours. When I first had my eyes opened to the multifarious delights of apple juice, it was largely skilful blends that caught my eye. In that first tasting there had been some juices of individual varieties, Duskin from Kent led the field with their Worcester, Bramley, Cox and Discovery, but these were the exceptions. The trend in the dawning of the golden age of apple juice is for declared varieties, either blended together in twos and threes or bottled individually.

At Marden, as the panel sniffed and sipped their way through the droves of juices under inspection, some clear winners eventually emerged, extraordinarily three out of the top four being made by the same farm, Dinmore in Herefordshire – a great feat in such a large blind tasting. The two closely related families who own Dinmore, the Davies and the Morleys only came into the apple juice business by mistake. Giving up careers in entirely different fields, they had bought the fruit farm – in rather a poor shape – in 1985 and had to dump ten tons of unsaleable eating fruit in their first year.

At the time they bought in apple juice from rival orchards to sell in their farm shop and it sold so well, they decided to go into production themselves using the 'graded out' fruit from their sixteen different apple tree varieties. They bought a small press and constructed their own bottle pasteuriser (processing only twenty-eight bottles at a time) from a washing boiler. Three thousand bottles were laboriously processed through this quaint device in their first year, with a handful being entered into the British Apple Juice Competition in Marden, triumphantly winning second place and giving the foursome enough confidence to expand their operation – and invent another pasteuriser, capable of holding 480 bottles this time.

Production last year was up to 30 000 bottles, way beyond their projections (15–20 000 had been their cautious estimate) and enough to whet the appetite of a major supermarket chain (though not quite sufficient volume to fill their order). That's one of the goals for the 1990s – to sell nationwide, although Angela Morley, devoted to her cottage industry, will consent to expansion on a grand scale only if she feels the 'home spun' quality can be retained.

Tasting the juices at the fruit show, it was all too apparent how things can go unpleasantly wrong. You can taste if any rotten fruit have slipped into the mix; tired, wrinkly fruit give a boiled sweet flavour; a 'peary' note creeps in if the fruit is insufficiently ripe; the juice can taste cooked if not treated properly; cidery, if time elapses before pasteurisation; overpressing gives a soapiness deriving from the skins. Apples have an elusive, delicate flavour and have to be treated carefully if they are to give of their best.

With their large number of different varieties on a smallish acreage, Dinmore started by blending different varieties throughout the season to fit their chosen categories: sweet, medium sweet and sharp. Early Discovery handles the sweet category alone until after Christmas, when Royalty takes a turn. Medium sweet rings the changes of the varieties throughout the year, but is dominated by Laxton Fortune and Bramley after Christmas. Bramleys inevitably dominate the sharp blend, with small quantities of 'softening' varieties blended in. A delicious Cox and Bramley blend is a constant.

Phillip Davies explained that it is a kind of juggling act, using the best fruit for the time of the year to give the best juice 'it all revolves around Bramley, which is the backbone'. All the apples are cold stored (rather than kept under gas – a crucial factor for quality, they think) and used in sequence of ripeness. His sister, Angela Morley, aware of the fashion for 'named varieties' is planning to move towards this on their labels, so if you become an apple juice snob, you'll know where you are.

Andrew Helbling (also a prize winner in the apple juice class I judged at Marden) has made the twelve single-variety Duskin apple juices since 1980, and again prides himself on his quaintly old-fashioned production methods, pressing the fruit – in tiny volumes for some of the more obscure varieties – in cloth. Tasting through his range of single varieties is an extraordinary voyage of discovery: you have the icing sugar sweetness of the Cox; the sharp, elusive twang of the Bramley; the fresh, true mirror image of the original apple in the Discovery; the tannic, almost chewy breadth of the Ellisson; and the rounder, apple-snow like softness of the James Grieve. The parallel with wines and the different grape varieties behind them is highlighted by this range; becoming clear as day when you look at the recent flux of apple wines made by English winemakers.

Poor English winemakers! Apart from a splendid burst of heat at the end of this decade, the weather was so unsuitable for their business, English winemaking virtually ground to a halt. Bill Ash of Staple Vineyards near Canterbury in Kent clammed up completely on the subject of the 1986 and 1987 harvests, 'I'd rather not talk about it,' he said. His wife told me that during these dreadful years, their grape yield slumped from an average of twenty-two tons to a miserable three tons; so Bill took a long hard look at all the equipment sitting unused in his winery and thought about what he could do with it. Apple wine seemed the answer, since this resilient fruit is less fazed by the weather than the fussier grapes. And based in the Orchard of Kent, there were plentiful supplies of runts of the litter graded out by local packhouses.

His Staple St James' apple wine is such a success that even when the vineyard is blessed by a bumper grape harvest, it'll be kept on as an established part of the Staple repertoire. To make it, essentially Bill treats the apples in exactly the same way as grapes, ('the juice can get a bit oxidised, but I don't worry about that, it gets cleared by fermentation anyway'). And he's found that a fifty/fifty blend of Bramleys and Cox's does the trick, giving a medium dry wine with a refreshing zip of acidity – at a very reasonable price. Producers making less than 10 000 bottles a year at an alcoholic strength of under 8.5 per cent pay negligible duty, pegging the price at £1.75–£1.95 a bottle.

I realised just how savagely the atrocious summers had bitten when I learnt that Lamberhurst, one of the largest English winemakers with 125 acres of grapes, is considering shifting the emphasis of their business towards apples. They grow a fair amount themselves and find buying in what they need for their two apple wines simpler than buying good grapes. Their latest apple wine, Special Reserve, is a whole new departure – a thunderbolt at near 15 per cent alcohol, sweetish in taste and spiritously alcoholic – a bit like apple brandy or calvados to taste, in fact.

Down in the West Country, deep into perry country (perry, of course, being the fermented juice of the pear) Three Choirs Vineyards in Newent, Gloucestershire consoled themselves after a run of poor harvests (unlike Kent, even 1988 was rotten for them) with the production of the traditional local tipple. Perry – real perry – is a very unusual drink, having the rich pungence of pears, but tasting dry – sometimes aggressively dry – and tannic, like old-fashioned red wines.

With grandiose intentions, Three Choirs have bulldozed terraces in the prime hillside sites on their farm to plant that most aristocratic of red grapes, the pinot noir. But in times of adversity, there their expensive equipment is, processing the tough-skinned perry pear. Eschewing the apple, winemaker Kit Morris feel more at home with pears, having made perry on a minute scale in the past to drink at home. And he, too, says making perry is similar to making wine – but considerably more hazardous; one slip and you've a vat of cider to dispose of. Gloster 'the winemaker's perry' is the product, in the slightly austere 'dry' style, aged in wood, and the more docile 'medium', softened by more evident fruit.

More and more English winemakers over the years have been considering entering the apple and pear wine and cider business (a master of the latter art is Biddenden Vineyard in Kent, who make a masterful Strong Kentish Cider), but there they meet the Catch 22. Robin Don, one of the old hands in the business making 48 000 bottles of the delicious Norfolk Apple wine a year explains that farm-scale production doesn't produce enough volume to interest supermarkets, BUT unless a product gets on to the supermarket shelves, it won't sell.

Most idiosyncratic apple juices and apple and pear wines are only available locally at present, from the farm gate and local delicatessens, but there are an increasing number to stretch the local zones out across the country, and signs that one or two may aspire to national distribution eventually.

Producers of apple and pear drinks

For your nearest stockist of the nectars mentioned in this chapter, contact the fruit farms.

Dinmore Apple Juice,
Dinmore Fruit Farm,
Dinmore,
Near Hereford
Telephone: 056 884 361.

Duskin Apple Juice,
Duskin Farm,
Kingston,
Near Canterbury
Telephone: 0227 830194.
For London stockists, contact Robertson's in Stoke Newington Church Street, London. Telephone: 01 254 3993.

Staple St James Apple Wine,
Staple Vineyards,
Church Farm,
Staple,
Canterbury
Telephone: 0304 812571.

Lamberhurst Vineyards,
Ridge Farm,
Near Tunbridge Wells
Telephone: 0892 890286.

Gloster Perry,
Three Choirs Vineyards,
Rhyle House,
Welsh House Lane,
Newent,
Gloucestershire
Telephone: 053 185 223.

Biddenden Cider,
Biddenden Vineyards,
Little Whatmans,
Biddenden,
Ashford, Kent
Telephone: 0580 291726.

Norfolk Apple Wine,
Hicks & Don Ltd,
Elmham,
Dereham,
Norfolk
Telephone: 036 281 571.

EAST MEETS WEST

INTRODUCTION
CHRIS KELLY

It had to happen sooner or later. The Prime Minister, Mrs Thatcher, has become an icon. Not in Sir Geoffrey Howe's private chapel or Grantham parish church, as you might expect, but in a Buddhist temple . . . in Wimbledon. Yet again fact trounces fiction; game, set and match.

The Buddha Padipa temple was inaugurated by Thailand's ruling monarchs in 1966. Heavy with gold leaf, it stands handsomely on a hill next to a small lake. Inside, the walls are covered with beautifully painted Thai frescoes. Not far from the large golden Buddha, on the left hand side, is a familiar figure among the images from Thai religion and mythology. Sure enough it is the Blessed Margaret, sitting rather primly in front of a hut, surveying the congregation. Next to her, for some obscure reason, lies a BBC clapperboard. Perhaps it was in honour of our visit.

We went for the annual festival of Loi Krathong. In Thailand it's held at the end of the rainy season, under a full moon. In Wimbledon things were different. We celebrated in the grey light of a freezing November Sunday. Apparently oblivious, the monks chanted in their thin saffron robes before leading us all to the nearby monastery for their only meal of the day; a feast prepared by the faithful. This was the ultimate in pot-luck, since the monks have no say in its preparation. Volunteers, who believe they are feeding the spirits of their dead ancestors, simply cook and serve whatever appeals to them. The monks must try every dish.

So, watched by their visitors, the monks knelt in silence while course after inventive course was presented. Serving on your knees (Buddhist custom required me to remain below the height of the revered guests) is a tricky business; especially for a six-foot Westerner with cartilage trouble. However, the offering clearly went down well. The monks consumed sticky rice; meat balls on skewers; bananas and rice cooked in leaves, and a dozen other imaginative and aromatic dishes with every sign of relish. I presented two sweet dishes (which you can find in this chapter). Occasionally they would pause and beam at the onlookers, who beamed back, delighted at their pleasure. Assuming that the diners knew little English, I was somewhat startled when the meal ended with a culture shock. As he passed me, one of the monks asked with a smile: 'Didn't you used to do that holiday programme?'

Outside, hardy stallholders were offering all manner of treats; freshly cooked meat or fish on skewers; the same banana-and-rice dish the monks had enjoyed so much; and a rich variety of exotic vegetables. Meanwhile, beside the temple, high-kicking Thai boxers were displaying a shaky grasp of charitable principles, and shivering beauties lined up bravely for the title Miss Thai Goosepimple 1988.

Towards sunset the good-humoured crowd drifted down to the lake. There we launched paper boats bearing lighted candles. My guide, Tippi, said the craft symbolised ignorance, greed and several other unworthy urges, which we were invited to shed. My candles went out almost at once. Shortly afterwards the boat capsized. I think the water goddess was trying to tell me something.

EAST MEETS NORTH-WEST

Ignorant and greedy as ever, I headed north to visit the site of a memorable *Food and Drink* challenge. We had asked Richard Shepherd of Langan's in London, to try his hand at Chinese cooking in the kitchens of the magnificent Yang Sing in Manchester. In 1983 it was voted the best Chinese restaurant in Britain. For my money, it's still at the top of the First Division. The highlight of our film was Richard's first traumatic encounter with the fierce heat that erupts from the Yang Sing's gas-fired range, under the woks. Imagine half a dozen Agas with Mount Etna inside and you'll have a rough idea of its intensity. The regulator has to be worked with the knee. Unfamiliar with the technique, Richard improvised a setting hitherto unknown in Oriental stove-technology. To 'HOT' and 'UNBELIEVABLY HOT' he added: '******* HELL!'

Shown the furnace by the Yang Sing's presiding genius, Harry Yeung, I understood how Richard felt. The raw flame is quite frighteningly powerful, and that, of course, is its secret. Nothing cooks in the woks for longer than three minutes, and many delicacies are dealt with much quicker. The giant steamers, like massive wall-safes, are fearsomely hot too. All in all, a Chinese kitchen is no place for the faint-hearted; nor is it a suitable refuge for the work-shy. In a busy day the Yang Sing will seat five hundred customers; most ordering around five courses; many on full-blown banquets. The roast chefs, dim sum chefs and wok chefs (the three main cooking categories), with their cutters, assistants, washers-up etc. put in ten and a half hour shifts and the pace is often frantic. Nevertheless the Yang Sing kitchen is orderly and spotless. The management boast that this is where Manchester's Environmental Health Officers come for their pre-Christmas dinner.

Born in Canton, Harry Yeung learnt the tough way. At the age of thirteen he began his apprenticeship in Hong Kong. Four years later he followed his father to Britain, working in London ('not very friendly') and Glasgow ('they don't even speak English there!') before settling in Manchester. In 1977 the Yeung family (including Harry's brother Gerry, a graduate of York University) founded the first Yang Sing in George Street, Manchester, moving to their present site, a former cotton warehouse in Princess Street, in 1985.

Harry's day starts early. By 6 am he's 'phoning the market, checking prices and availability. With a food budget of several thousand pounds a week, he's a much-prized customer. He's also a hard man to beat when it comes to haggling. Manchester, however, can't satisfy all his needs, so once a year he goes back to Hong Kong for the ingredients only the East can provide. Then he fills two containers with dried exotica, including sharks' fins (like great off-white antlers); freshwater wheat (bearing a disturbing resemblance to large, black Brillo pads); cows' tendon; sea cucumber (actually sea slug, but 'cucumber' sounds more acceptable to sensitive Western ears); black moss (like sooty tree-bark); and abalone. Given his head, Harry would add authentic delicacies such as snake. The British palate, however, isn't quite ready for royal python in black bean sauce, and in any case you need a licence to import them.

Inspecting the stores above the Yang Sing was a fascinating

experience. The range of possibilities – of flavours and textures – at the command of a talented Chinese chef is almost limitless. It makes the European repertoire look distinctly under-privileged. Better still, however, was the proof of the pudding. For lunch Harry pulled out all the Cantonese stops. There were rice rolls (smooth, white rice pancakes with delicious beef and prawn fillings); soup dumplings (the delicately flavoured soup is revealed when you puncture the dumpling); prawn and meat dumplings; tiny, tender spare ribs with garlic sauce; steamed whelks in a satay sauce; goose webs (the feet of geese, marinated in stock containing spicy seeds; they might sound off-putting but they taste excellent); crunchy filaments of jellyfish; smooth, creamy cuttlefish; dover sole with *al dente* asparagus and straw mushrooms; pig's tongue, subtly marinated; suckling pig with a crispy skin; and beef on a hot plate in a rich, fruity sauce.

The Yang Sing positively encourages its customers not to make their minds up; at least not too soon. Harry likes them to arrive with their options open; discuss that day's specials with the cheerful and immensely helpful staff; and literally create the meal at the table. The choice can be almost overwhelming. On Sundays, for instance, there are some sixty varieties of dim sum on offer, and Harry is constantly inventing new temptations. His only handicap is our timidity.

Restaurants of the Yang Sing's quality are consciously trying to upgrade the perception of Chinese food in Britain. They're motivated partly by the desire to make more people aware of the extraordinary versatility of one of the world's great cuisines, and partly by more mundane considerations. Chinese staff are increasingly hard to come by, due to tightening immigration procedures, and second generation British Chinese are not eager to base careers in an industry with a take-away image. Long live the Yang Sing's initiative. Evidence of its success is that you'll need to book five weeks ahead for a table there on a Saturday night. If you can't wait that long then try some of the recipes Richard Shepherd had to cook . . .

RECIPES
MICHAEL BARRY

I'm not sure what impressed me most about the Yang Sing, Richard Shepherd's courage in making the journey (and learning so much from it too), or the extreme simplicity of the dishes when you saw them being made. On more than one occasion Richard couldn't believe that the ingredients he was faced with were all that were needed. A useful Far Eastern reminder of Escoffier's great cooking maxim: 'fait simple' – keep it simple! Here are two recipes which do just that.

BEEF WITH CHILLI, PEPPER AND BLACK BEAN SAUCE
Serves 4

For the marinade:
1 tablespoon custard powder
2 tablespoons water
1 egg

1 lb (450 g) beef fillet steak, thinly sliced
1 tablespoon black beans, dried or soft (from Chinese supermarkets)
1 clove garlic, crushed
Oil for frying
1½ teaspoons chopped fresh ginger root
1 teaspoon sugar
Peel from 1 tangerine, cut into fine threads and soaked in hot water
(or 1 teaspoon of dried from a Chinese supermarket)
1 glass Chinese cooking wine or dry white wine
1 green pepper, chopped
A pinch of hot chilli pepper or ½ teaspoon fresh chilli, chopped
1 spring onion, chopped into 1-in (2.5-cm) lengths
1 tablespoon chicken stock
1 teaspoon oyster sauce (available in jars)
1 teaspoon dark soy sauce
1 teaspoon salt
1 teaspoon potato starch or cornflour mixed with a little water

Mix the marinade ingredients and stir into the meat. Leave while you prepare the rest of the dish.

Fry the black beans and garlic in a little oil for 30 seconds. Add the ginger, sugar, drained tangerine peel (or dried) and half of the wine. Cook for 1 minute. Remove from the wok. If using dried black beans, steam them for 20 to 30 minutes until tender. (If using fresh/soft beans there is no need to steam them.) When the beans are cooked, you can cook the rest of the ingredients.

Add a little more oil to the wok and stir-fry the beef, then remove it from the wok when cooked. Next fry the pepper, chilli and spring onion. Return the bean mixture to the wok and fry for 1 minute. Return the beef, and add the chicken stock, oyster sauce, soy sauce and remaining wine. Add the salt and taste for seasoning. Thicken with the potato starch or cornflour mixed with a little water. Serve.

YEUNG CHOW FRIED RICE
Serves 4

1 tablespoon corn oil
2 eggs, beaten
1 lb (450 g) cooked rice
1 teaspoon salt
1 teaspoon soy sauce
1 oz (25 g) prawns, cooked and peeled
1 oz (25 g) roast pork or ham, diced
1 spring onion, chopped
Small handful chopped iceberg lettuce

Heat the oil in a wok or frying pan and fry the eggs. Then add the cooked rice, salt and soy sauce. Stir-fry, add the prawns and pork, stir-fry, then add the spring onion and lettuce. Serve.

THAI RECIPES
I recently spent some time in Thailand studying the cooking – so it was a pleasure for me to see the festival Chris visited and to watch the excellent Thai restaurants spread across Britain in the last couple of years. These two pudding recipes may seem a little unusual at first but you only need a taste of one to be half way to Bangkok. Bon voyage, with one of the delicious sweets to complement the journey.

MANGO WITH STICKY RICE
Serves 6

10 oz (275 g) sticky rice
8 fl oz (250 ml) thick tinned coconut milk
2 tablespoons sugar
½ teaspoon salt
3 ripe mangoes
2 tablespoons coconut cream

Sticky rice is bought by that name and is available in oriental and specialist stores. To make it, soak the rice in cold water for 3 hours. Drain and rinse. Line the perforated part of a steamer with a double thickness of muslin and turn the rice on to it. Steam the rice over a medium heat for 30 minutes. In a saucepan or heatproof bowl, mix the coconut milk, sugar and salt; heat until the sugar has dissolved. Mix in the still warm rice, and set aside for 30 minutes. Peel the mangoes, and slice the two 'cheeks' of each fruit as close to the stone as possible. Slice each piece into 4 pieces lengthways. Mound the rice in the centre of a serving dish and arrange the slices of mango around it. Pour the coconut cream over the rice and serve.

GOLDEN THREADS
Serves 4

1 lb (450 g) sugar
16 fl oz (475 ml) water
6 egg yolks

Make a syrup with the sugar and water. Have a warmed serving dish ready. Strain the egg yolks through a piece of muslin over a bowl, any egg white left in the eggs should remain in the muslin. Put the egg in an icing bag with a very small nozzle (⅛ in/3 mm). Bring the sugar syrup to a simmer. Carefully trickle and swirl the egg yolks into the syrup, making a spiral about 2 in (5 cm) in diameter, leaving a small hole in the middle. Make the spirals one at a time. Insert a skewer into the hole in the middle, swirl and lift out folding the golden threads onto the serving dish. They will keep for several days.

SATAY AND SATAY SAUCE
Serves 4

A possible companion to your Thai meal would be to serve sticks of Satay. Bamboo skewers of tiny pieces of chicken, lamb or occasionally beef, these originally came from Indonesia, but have proved one of the world's universally popular dishes now eaten all over South-East Asia, and wherever South-East Asian food is liked. There are many different marinades and versions of the sauce that is used to dip the mini kebabs in. The one I love best is close to the Javanese original, rich with coconut and peanut flavour.

For the satay:
1 lb (450 g) chicken breast, lamb or beef fillet
4 tablespoons soy sauce
1 clove garlic, crushed
2 tablespoons soft brown sugar
2 tablespoons lemon or lime juice

For the sauce:
4 tablespoons desiccated coconut
⅓ pint (200 ml) hot water
6 tablespoons crunchy peanut butter
2 teaspoons chilli sauce

Cut the meat into pieces the size of a large postage stamp and marinate in the next 4 ingredients for 2 hours. Thread on pointed bamboo skewers – 5 to a skewer – threaded flat. Grill under a *hot* grill for 3 minutes each side.

To make the sauce, soak the coconut in the hot water for 30 minutes. Work with a fork or your hands. Add to all the other sauce ingredients in a saucepan and then add all the marinade, after using the meat. Stir and bring to a gentle boil. The sauce will cook to a beautiful glossy brown. Serve with raw cucumber slices and cold rice cakes for authenticity.

CHICKEN TIKKA
Serves 4

This is a classic Indian grilled chicken dish. Now eaten throughout the subcontinent, it originated in the north-west near the Afghan border. It has some of the excitement of its nomadic past still attached, especially if eaten with the flat Indian bread and the yoghurt chutneys I've suggested.

6 skinned breasts of chicken cut into smallish pieces

For the marinade:
5 oz (150 g) plain yoghurt
½ Spanish onion, sliced
Juice of ½ lemon
2-3 cloves of garlic, chopped
2 teaspoons turmeric
2 teaspoons ground cumin seed
1 teaspoon ground or fresh ginger
1½ teaspoons chilli powder
2 good teaspoons ground coriander
2 bay leaves

Mix the marinade ingredients together in a large bowl. Add the chicken pieces and leave in the refrigerator for 6 hours or longer. Pre-heat the oven to 450°F (230°C), gas mark 8. Lift the chicken pieces out of the marinade, removing large pieces of onion that might have stuck to the chicken, and place on a raised wire rack over a baking tray. Sprinkle with a little salt and bake in a very hot oven for 30 to 40 minutes until brown and crisp on the outside and soft in the middle. Serve with sliced lettuce, lemon quarters and caramelised onions and chutneys.

To caramelise onions, simply slice them and then fry them in very hot oil until crispy. Keep stirring or the onions will burn.

CRAFTY YOGHURT CHUTNEY

5 oz (150 g) plain yoghurt
2-in (5-cm) piece of cucumber, grated
2 teaspoons concentrated mint sauce

Mix all the ingredients and leave for 30 minutes before using.

PARATHAS
Makes 4

6 oz (175 g) wholewheat or 'Attar' flour
1 teaspoon salt
Scant ½ pint (300 ml) warm water
2 oz (50 g) butter

Mix the flour, salt and water together to form a soft dough. The quantity of water will depend on a number of factors including the weather, so add it bit by bit. Divide into 4 balls. Roll each out 8 in (20 cm) across and butter. Fold into 4 and roll out again – a fan shape ¼-in (5-mm) thick is the end result. Cook on a hot dry griddle or thick frying pan for approximately 4 minutes each side, until browned and with blisters forming. Keep them warm in a tea towel while you finish the rest.

VEGETARIAN COUSCOUS
Serves 4

A dish from the Magreb, the western end of Arabia spread across the top of Africa, couscous is almost the national dish of Tunisia, Morocco and Algeria. Each area and often town has its own version – fishy or fiery, mild or muttony, this vegetarian version is from Morocco and uses the traditional seven vegetables in a luscious rich stew to go with the delicate rice-like, steamed, cracked wheat. You can buy couscous grain in any supermarket these days by the way – a real sign of progress!

1 lb (450 g) couscous
2 large onions
8 oz (225 g) courgettes
8 oz (225 g) green beans
8 oz (225 g) carrots
1 small cauliflower, broken into florets
8 oz (225 g) cooked or tinned chick peas
1 teaspoon turmeric
½ teaspoon cinnamon
2 teaspoons salt
1 clove garlic, crushed
1 oz (25 g) butter

Put the couscous in a bowl, add 2 cups of tepid water and mix with a fork. The couscous will rapidly absorb the liquid and begin to swell; use the fork to prevent large lumps forming. In a large pan place all the vegetables, cut into large pieces, add the spices and garlic and cover with 1 in (2.5 cm) of water. (Alternately you could fry the onions first in some olive oil to soften them and enrich the dish, before adding the other vegetables.) Bring gently to the boil, put the couscous in a metal sieve or colander and place over the cooking vegetables, cover with a tight fitting lid (use a tea towel for extra sealing if you like) and let the couscous cook over the steam. Cook for about 25 to 30 minutes. Stir the butter into the cooked couscous and spoon it out on to a large plate. Make a well in the middle and spoon in the vegetables, reserving the stock. Moisten the couscous with a little stock. Reserve some of the cooking juices to make the hot delicious sauce – Harissa. (So named, in my opinion, because it is so hot it forces an expletive much like 'Harissa!' out of you.)

HARISSA
Serves 4

8 fl oz (250 ml) stock from the cooked vegetables
2 garlic cloves, crushed
1 teaspoon chilli powder
½ teaspoon ground cumin

Mix all the ingredients together and serve alongside the couscous.

FIVE INDIAN DISHES FOR A FEAST FOR EIGHT

Indian food is a very complex subject. It varies from one end of the subcontinent to the other, as much as Greek and Danish or Italian and Scottish food does. And it isn't made up of 'curries' – at least except where British influence still reigns supreme – more parts of the area than you might suppose. Here then are five dishes from across India which can be eaten together, or any two of which, with rice, will make a delicious meal for four. Vegetarian, fish or meat-based as you choose. Yoghurt with sliced cucumber, good chutney and some crisp popadoms are ideal accompaniments.

CHANA DHALL

A rich dish of solid pulses that is mild in flavour.

1 onion, chopped
1 clove garlic, chopped
1-in (2.5-cm) piece of ginger, peeled and chopped
2 tablespoons oil
1 tablespoon turmeric
½ teaspoon chilli powder
8 oz (225 g) chick peas, soaked for 6 hours
1 pint (600 ml) water
2 tablespoons plain yoghurt
Salt

Fry the onion, garlic and ginger in the oil for 2 minutes. Add the turmeric, chilli and chick peas, and stir for 1 minute. Add the water, bring to the boil, and simmer for 1 to 1½ hours until the chick peas are tender. The water should be almost all absorbed; if not boil briskly until dry. Stir in the yoghurt, season generously with salt and serve.

KEEMA AND PEAS

In a country where the tenderness of the meat can leave a lot to be desired and hanging – before refrigeration – was hardly an option, mince became the answer (as I explained in Chapter 9). This is easy, delicious and can at a pinch be made with a mild curry powder.

2 tablespoons oil
1 lb (450 g) onions, chopped
3 cloves garlic, chopped
1 teaspoon coriander
1 teaspoon cumin
1 teaspoon turmeric
1 teaspoon ginger
1 lb (450 g) lamb or beef mince
12 fl oz (350 ml) water
1 teaspoon black pepper
1 teaspoon salt
1 tablespoon brown sugar
1 tablespoon lemon juice
½ teaspoon cinnamon
½ teaspoon nutmeg
8 oz (225 g) frozen or fresh peas

Heat the oil and fry the onion and garlic until well browned. Add the first 4 spices and fry for a further 2 minutes. Put in the meat and fry, breaking it up with a wooden spoon until browned. Add the water and simmer for 30 minutes. Add all the other ingredients, stir and simmer for 5 minutes. (If the peas are fresh they will need 12 minutes to cook not 5.)

BENGALI FISH

Though hardly ever seen in our Indian restaurants, fish are highly prized and much eaten in these countries with thousands of miles of coasts (and some of the greatest rivers in the world).

2 tablespoons oil
8 oz (225 g) onions, peeled and sliced
1 clove garlic, chopped
1 teaspoon ground ginger
1 teaspoon cumin
1 teaspoon cinnamon
8 fl oz (250 ml) water
½ teaspoon chilli
½ teaspoon black pepper
½ teaspoon salt
1 lb (450 g) white fish fillets (haddock, cod or coley), cut into 4 pieces
1 tablespoon brown sugar
1 tablespoon lemon juice

Heat the oil and fry the onions and garlic until well browned. Add the ginger, cumin and cinnamon and fry for a further 2 minutes. Add the water and simmer while you rub the chilli, pepper and salt on the fish. Put the fish in the sauce and spoon over. Cook for 10 to 15 minutes until the fish is cooked through. Take out the fish pieces and boil the sauce with the sugar and lemon for 2 minutes. Pour over the fish and serve.

CHICKEN KORMA

2 oz (50 g) butter
8 oz (225 g) onions, thinly sliced
1 clove garlic, chopped
2 bay leaves
1 stick cinnamon
4 cloves   (These are all *whole*
8 peppercorns   spices not *ground*.)
4 cardamon pods
1 teaspoon salt
4 chicken breasts
10 oz (275 g) plain yoghurt
2 oz (50 g) ground almonds
Milk

Melt the butter and fry the onions and garlic gently for 15 minutes. Mix all the other ingredients except the chicken and almonds. Cut the chicken breasts in half crossways. Marinate the chicken breasts in the yoghurt for 10 minutes, then add the chicken and yoghurt to the onions, cover and cook gently for 40 minutes, stirring occasionally. Mix the almonds with a little milk and stir into the sauce. Bring to the boil and serve.

EGG AND POTATO BHAJI

No, not a subcontinental fried egg and chips but a bright and vivid-tasting casserole that traditionally uses duck eggs though chickens' eggs taste great too.

2 tablespoons oil
8 oz (225 g) onions, thinly sliced
1 clove garlic
1 dessertspoon ginger
1 dessertspoon cumin
1 dessertspoon turmeric
1 teaspoon chilli powder (or less to taste)
1 × 8-oz (225-g) tin Italian tomatoes
6 hard-boiled eggs
6 egg-sized new potatoes, scrubbed and boiled for 5 minutes
Salt
Coriander or parsley, chopped

Heat the oil and fry the onions and garlic until browned, add the spices and fry for 2 minutes more. Put in the tomatoes and their juice and mash with a fork until blended. Cover and simmer for 25 minutes. Halve the eggs and potatoes and place in the sauce. Simmer together for 10 minutes, salt and serve. Chopped coriander or parsley sprinkled over the dish before serving looks pretty and tastes good.

THE BEST OF BRITISH

A TRIBUTE TO MICHAEL SMITH

INTRODUCTION
CHRIS KELLY

Michael Smith died on 20 January 1989, aged 61, and many of his friends still haven't forgiven him. He was so full of energy, humour and generosity, it's hard to believe he's no longer among us. His open, giving nature was a rarity, especially in an era when to show warmth is to be suspected of weakness or, worse, lack of naked ambition.

Michael was neither weak nor unambitious. His physical drive was formidable. Although his health had been far from robust for many years, he consistently set himself a punishing schedule. Getting up at 5.30 am he would have written numerous memos, letters, pieces for various publications, or notes for a new book by the time most of us were ready for the first shot of caffeine. If the telephone rang before breakfast, we always knew who it was. From then until he started to wilt at around 11 pm he would be in top gear; an eternal enthusiast who couldn't bear to waste a precious moment.

As for ambitions, I think he had three. Above all he wanted to see his family secure and happy. He aimed to give his utmost to every project in which he was involved; to achieve the best he could. And he cared passionately about restoring the status of British cuisine. His professional life was largely devoted to that end – on television, in print and in person – and he won a good many battles, if not the war.

Michael was born into a solid, middle class Yorkshire Methodist family – the youngest of six children. His father was a textile manufacturer and they were 'middling-well-off'. As he explained in his preface to *Afternoon Tea* (Macmillan): 'The household consisted of my mother and father, two brothers and three sisters, two live-in maids, a nanny, a charlady and a general factotum. None of these servants were the luxury they may sound to us nowadays; they were a necessity in a household where every stitch of linen was laundered and ironed by the maids and my sisters, and every loaf of bread, every cake and biscuit, pie, pound of jam or marmalade was made by my mother and her helpers.' With that background it was hardly surprising that Michael's loyalties lay with our native tradition of cooking.

Nevertheless his first dreams were of stage design. There wasn't much call for that in Leeds, however, so he settled for catering. Opting, typically, for the best, his father sent him to the International Hotel School in Lausanne, where Michael marvelled at the opulent contrasts to the deprivations of post-War Britain. Next came a period at the Palace Hotel, Copenhagen, where he was very happy, and a spell in Paris, where he wasn't. And so back home to Leeds, managing three hotels.

Soon, travel and experience gave Michael the confidence to open his own place, Foxhill, outside the city. In this Victorian mansion he started putting his ideas into practice with the help of his wife Elisabeth. And those ideas underwent a dramatic sea-change when he came by a 200 year-old book: *The Experienced English Housekeeper* by Elizabeth Raffald. Here was the signpost Michael had needed. It set him on a British road from which he never deviated. The benefits of his conversion were also felt at nearby Harewood House where he was invited to prepare banquets.

Bought out by Crockfords, the Smiths moved from Foxhill back into Leeds with The Kitchen, the forerunner of today's proliferating cookshops, with a restaurant attached. Later Michael remembered hopeful callers like Laura Ashley, trying to sell her tea towels. The business was ahead of its time, however. Yorkshire was no more ready for sophisticated kitchen equipment than it had been for theatre design.

His flair for the latter was to come into its own when Michael moved to London. Friends from Yorkshire asked him to design a fashionable Knightsbridge restaurant, Walton's, for them. (He was actually eating there when IRA bombers later made it their target.) For the same team he designed The English House and

The English Garden, also advising on all aspects of cooking and presentation.

There followed reams of journalism (including a long association with *Homes and Gardens*); many books (among them the highly influential *Fine English Cookery* and *New English Cookery*); countless television appearances (Pebble Mill, Daytime Live, the *Food and Drink Quiz et al*); food design and consultancy on the small screen (*Upstairs, Downstairs* and *The Duchess of Duke Street*); and numerous other food-related enterprises.

I was lucky enough to share one of Michael's last projects with him. He knew that Hans Schweitzer and I wanted to open a restaurant in Cambridge. When he came to stay one weekend, we showed him a site we had in mind: Midsummer House, which stands in a walled garden by the river. At once, without a second's hesitation, he said: 'Buy it, Monday morning. I'll come in with you.' We did. He did. It proved to be a happy, fruitful, and all too brief partnership. Michael galvanised everyone involved with his energy and total commitment. He worked tirelessly to create an English country house look which perfectly complements the setting and the cuisine. He's greatly missed.

It was entirely typical of Michael's attention to detail that he left meticulous instructions in his will about the arrangements for his cremation and memorial service, if there were to be one (as indeed there was). After the ordeal at the crematorium the mourners were to be given sandwiches made with farmhouse-cured Yorkshire ham. He even named the species of lily he thought suitable to decorate St James', Piccadilly, where the subsequent service was held. It was all tongue in cheek, of course. Michael never took himself seriously; was never pompous. His tastes were both simple and extravagant, but never pretentious. He believed in giving life all you've got, and having a laugh while you're about it. To borrow a title from his fellow Yorkshireman, J. B. Priestley, this uncomplicated philosophy made Michael Smith one of the all-time good companions.

RECIPES
MICHAEL BARRY

Over the last twenty-five years, Michael Smith was a cornerstone in the rebirth of English cookery. No that's wrong – Michael Smith *is* one of *the* cornerstones in the rebirth of English cookery. All the young brilliant chefs of the last two or three years, building their reputations on the robust flavours and independent sauces of their versions of English food, owe more than they know to Michael. Trained to cook in the most rigorous classical manner in that most rigorous of traditional countries – Switzerland – he returned to his native Yorkshire (as Chris explained) in the 1950s and began to present and delight in dishes traditional to that county and to Britain. He researched through history libraries and country houses, great and small, and cooked what he discovered with skill and panache. He finally broke on to the national scene with the stunning food that made the TV series of *Upstairs, Downstairs* and *The Duchess of Duke Street*, culinary as well as dramatic masterpieces. Then followed many series of TV programmes notably from Pebble Mill where with *Grace and Flavour* and *Posh Nosh* he taught us all how to achieve the renaissance of English food.

Towards the end of his life, however, he changed his approach. The frontispiece of his *New English Cookery*, a significant title, says, 'I reserve the right to change my ideas in the light of new experiences in my life.' Always in the past by his own admission 'a cream with everything man', he now felt the need for a little more lightness and delicacy – for a healthier pattern of eating. In selecting some of my favourites among his recipes I was struck by how much his style of cooking had changed and how little his own personal style. As always, old or new recipes, he was humorous, enthusiastic, devoted to skills and flavours, generous and most poignantly, life-enhancing.

STARTERS

Four starters ranging from one of his favourite textured soups through to a piece of medieval cookery research that became a restaurant favourite.

MUSHROOM, TOMATO, ORANGE AND WALNUT SOUP
Serves 4 to 6
Dark-toned and tweedy in texture, this is an ideal main course soup.

12 oz (350 g) flat black-cap mushrooms
1 oz (25 g) butter or oil
1 clove garlic, crushed
Up to 1 pint (600 ml) rich beef stock, or chicken stock
2 fl oz (50 ml) Amontillado sherry
½ pint (300 ml) tomato pulp made from 1 lb (450 g) tomatoes,
skinned, seeded and roughly chopped
¼ pint (150 ml) fresh orange juice
¼ teaspoon finely grated orange rind
Salt and milled white pepper to taste

For the garnish:
1 orange, segmented with a knife
1 tomato, skinned, seeded and cut into petals
2 oz (50 g) walnuts, toasted, lightly salted and roughly crushed
(These can all be made a day in advance.)

Trim the stalk ends and peel the mushrooms. Chop roughly. Melt the butter or oil in a heavy-bottomed pan until foaming and almondy. Add the mushrooms and garlic, toss well and stir over a brisk heat until the juices begin to draw. Add all the remaining ingredients, lower the heat, and simmer for 15 to 20 minutes. Allow to cool before blending – but do not over-blend; a somewhat tweedy texture is preferable. Re-heat and serve with a little of each garnish stirred into each cup.

CHAMPIGNONS GRATINÉS
(MUSHROOMS GLAZED WITH CHEESE)
Makes 8 to 10 cocottes
This simple yet rich dish was possibly the most effective I ever produced from the kitchens of Foxhill and later The Kitchen in Leeds.

Even to this day I will meet a former 'bride' at some luncheon club lecture or other who will say 'Do you remember serving that mushroom dish at my wedding?' Of course I do. It was in such demand that there was hardly an elegant wedding, twenty-first or other buffet party where it didn't make its entrance, dressed in a cocotte standing on a d'oylied saucer with a teaspoon for ease of eating and served on huge silver trays direct from the kitchens.

Here's the original recipe twenty-eight years later! It will make eight to ten cocottes depending on their size.

1 lb (450 g) crisp white tight-capped button mushrooms
2 oz (50 g) butter
1 pint (600 ml) double cream
2½ fl oz (65 ml) brandy
Salt and freshly milled white or black pepper
4 oz (100 g) Parmesan or Gruyère cheese, grated

Finely slice the mushrooms. In a large pan melt the butter until foaming and giving off a nutty smell. Fry the mushrooms for 1 to 2 minutes. Pour over the cream and brandy. Season lightly with salt and pepper. Cook for 2 to 3 minutes. Take out the mushrooms with a draining spoon. Reduce the cream by boiling rapidly until it is thick. (If the sauce appears oily add a spoonful of boiling water to restore the emulsion.) Bring the mushrooms and sauce together, fill into small cocottes, sprinkle liberally with the grated cheese and brown under a spanking hot grill.

This dish can be made successfully a day in advance, in which case allow the mushroom mixture to cool completely before filling into cocottes and sprinkling with the cheese. Pre-heat the oven to 450°F (230°C), gas mark 8. Stand the cocottes on a baking tray and bake in the oven until they are browned on top and bubbling – this will take about 15 minutes.

If, at a buffet party, the guests are tardy, lower the temperature to 225°F (110°C), gas mark ¼. The cocottes will sit happily waiting for 30 minutes or so, but not much longer as the cheese, particularly if you have used Gruyère, tends to toughen.

POTTED TONGUE
Serves 6 to 8

This recipe also makes an excellent 'dip' if worked into a soft paste and then gently mixed with single cream (about ¼ pint (150 ml)) until it is of a dippable consistency.

8 oz (225 g) ox tongue, tinned or home-cooked
3 oz (75 g) good butter
1 tablespoon Demerara or Jamaica rum
¼ teaspoon black pepper
1 teaspoon mild Dijon mustard
NB No salt
Clarified butter

Simply blend everything except the clarified butter together in a machine. If you don't possess a machine, mince, or finely chop, the tongue and pound the other ingredients in a metal bowl using the butt of a rolling pin. (I sometimes mix into the paste 4 oz (100 g) of tongue cut into tiny cubes, to give added texture.) Pack the mixture into 1 large or 6 small individual pots. Level the surface and float over a thin film of clarified butter. Put to set in the refrigerator.

Serve with hot crisp brown toast using the butter from the top of the tongue to spread. Extra butter can be to hand for those liking a lot on their toast.

TARTE DE BRY
Serves 6 to 8

My meeting with Lorna J. Sass from The Metropolitan Museum in New York City stimulated my interest in medieval cookery. A visit with her to our own British Museum to peruse that most famous of all culinary manuscripts, the *Forme of Cury*, from which much of her first book, *To the King's Taste*, on the feasts and recipes of the court of Richard II is based, prompted me to look into this area myself. Hitherto I had been engrossed by the seventeenth and eighteenth centuries.

This tarte has proved one of the most popular dishes on the menu of The English House. It is simple to make, being executed in exactly the same way as a quiche. It is best served hot, straight from the oven whilst it is still somewhat puffed up. I squeeze a little unsalted butter over the surface of the baked tart to make it even more appetising.

8 oz (225 g) medium ripe Brie cheese
1 clove garlic, crushed
Juice of ½ lemon
Salt and freshly milled white pepper
1 shortcrust flan case, baked blind
4 whole eggs
1 egg yolk
½ pint (300 ml) milk
½ pint (300 ml) single cream

Pre-heat the oven to 325°F (160°C), gas mark 3. Cut the cheese into ¼-in (5-mm) cubes, and toss with the crushed garlic in the lemon juice. Season with salt and pepper. Disperse evenly over the base of the flan case.

Beat the eggs and yolk. Season well with salt and pepper. Bring the milk and cream to boiling point and pour over the eggs, whisking all the time. Pour this mixture into the flan case and bake in the oven until the custard is just set and is light and fluffy – about 45 to 50 minutes.

MAIN COURSES

Ranging from delicate creamy confections of salmon trout to his version of a good shepherd's pie . . . Michael Smith's recipes all show an enthusiasm for letting the ingredients shine through. I've included some specific contrasts: an old and new steak and kidney recipe showing the move to lightness so clearly. You might also like to compare the chicken recipes, or the two trouts. As he said, 'here are rich and poor recipes, polysaturated and unsaturated, expensive and cheap, as I . . . found things in my life.'

HOT PÂTÉ OF SALMON TROUT
Serves 6 to 8

1¼ lb (500 g) salmon trout, skinned and boned weight
4 eggs plus 2 yolks, beaten
1 pint (600 ml) double cream, well chilled
Salt and freshly milled white pepper
Butter
Fronds of fresh dill

Cut the fish into 1-in (2.5-cm) cubes. In a food processor or blender make a fine purée of the fish, gradually adding the eggs as you progress. Transfer this mixture to a large mixing bowl and put to chill for at least 2 hours.

When you are ready to make up the pâté remove the fish purée and the cream from the fridge and gradually beat in the cream a bit at a time, adding a little salt and pepper as you go along (this quantity will take about a level teaspoonful of salt). The consistency of the mixture when all the cream is incorporated should be just about that of a Victoria sponge mix, i.e. dropping consistency.

Pre-heat the oven to 400°F (200°C), gas mark 6. Butter a 2-lb (1-kg) seamless loaf tin or other deep receptacle (a ring mould is excellent for this). Lay 3 or 4 fronds of dill in the bottom. Spoon the mixture into the buttered mould, giving the mould a good hard bang on the table top to settle the mixture into the corners. Smooth over the top with the back of a wetted spoon. Cover with a piece of buttered foil, sealing it well round the edges and, if your mould is fairly full, making a good 1-in (2.5-cm) pleat along the top. Stand the mould in a roasting tin of hot water, coming half way up its sides. Cook in the oven, on the centre shelf for 50 minutes.

Unmould on to a warm serving dish. Mop away any wet which may be present with paper kitchen towels. Cut into ½-in (1-cm) slices and coat one half with fresh sherried tomato purée (below) and the other with Hollandaise Sauce.

For high days and holidays this dish can be made even richer by adding a layer of cubes of salmon trout as follows:

1 lb (450 g) extra salmon trout cut into ½-in (1-cm) cubes
1 cup dry white wine
1 small onion, finely sliced
1 large frond of dill
A little salt and milled white pepper

Marinate the salmon in the wine, onion and herbs for an hour. Discard the marinade. Spread half the raw fish purée in the buttered mould, distributing the marinated salmon cubes evenly. Spread over the second half of the purée, then cook as directed above.

PAN-FRIED TROUT WITH TWO HERBS
Serves 4

4 × 8–10 oz (225–275 g) trout, gutted and headed
Salt and milled pepper
Lemon juice
12–18 sage leaves
4 small sprigs fresh thyme
Flour for dredging
3 tablespoons olive or soy oil
1 oz (25 g) butter
Chive butter

Season the inside of each trout with salt, pepper and a good squeeze of lemon juice. Fill with the sage leaves and thyme sprigs. Dredge the trout lightly with seasoned flour on both sides. Heat the oil and butter in a large frying pan, swirl around until the butter is evenly melted and beginning to brown slightly. Fry the trout over a medium to high heat for 10 minutes, turning them about every 2 minutes. The trout are cooked when the flesh gives when pressed gently in the thickest part with the tip of a forefinger. Drain, and serve with a spoonful of chive butter.

FRESH TOMATO PURÉE

1 lb (450 g) tomatoes, skinned, deseeded and chopped
1 dessertspoon dry sherry
¼ pint (150 ml) tomato juice
1 level teaspoon caster sugar
1 large sprig dill (or mint)
1 dessertspoon lemon juice
Salt and milled white pepper

Put all the ingredients into an enamel pan and simmer to a fine pulp. Press through a fine sieve, re-heat and serve.

CHICKEN CREAMS IN SHRIMP SAUCE

Serves 6

The quantity given will make six creams in moulds which are 3 in (7.5 cm) in diameter. Butter the moulds well. This recipe shoots up-market when Mediterranean prawns are used. Allow four prawns per serving, otherwise proceed as directed.

For the sauce:

4 oz (100 g) fresh shrimps (or frozen in shells) or Mediterranean prawns
1 baby onion
1 oz (25 g) butter
½ oz (15 g) plain flour
1 teaspoon paprika
1 clove garlic, crushed
1 level teaspoon tomato purée
½ pint (300 ml) boiling water
¼ pint (150 ml) thick cream
1 teaspoon lemon juice
Salt and pepper

2 eggs
½ pint (300 ml) double cream, chilled
10 oz (275 g) raw chicken breast when skinned and boned
Salt and pepper
A touch of nutmeg

First prepare the sauce. Shell the shrimps and put them on one side; retain the heads and shells. Chop the onion and soften this in the melted butter in a small pan. Sprinkle with the flour and stir well in; add the paprika, garlic and tomato purée. Pour on the boiling water and bring the sauce to the boil again. Add the cream and simmer for 2 minutes; add the shrimp shells and heads, cover the pan with a lid and, over the lowest possible heat, simmer the sauce for 20 minutes, stirring occasionally to prevent any sticking.

Strain the sauce through a fine sieve into a basin. Wash out the pan and return the sauce to it. Season with lemon juice, salt and pepper (it may be salty enough, so take care). Don't add the shrimps at this stage or they will toughen. Cover the surface of the sauce with a circle of buttered paper and stand the pan in a larger pan of hot water to keep warm.

Before making the chicken creams, make sure that you have a baking dish large enough to contain either castle pudding moulds or individual soufflé dishes. Failing this, small straight-sided coffee cups work very well – or the whole cream can be made in a ring mould.

Beat the eggs. Chill the cream in the refrigerator. Skin and wipe the chicken, and put it first through the fine blade of the mincer and then, with the beaten eggs, through a blender or mouli, making as fine a purée as you can. Chill this well and then gradually beat the cream little by little into the purée, adding a little salt if it looks as though it is getting too thin. You will notice that the mixture 'seizes' and thickens when you do this, but take care to be quite modest with the salt. Add a little pepper. When all the cream is incorporated, you should have a mixture which is just about dropping consistency.

Pre-heat the oven to 400°F (200°C), gas mark 6. Two-thirds fill the baking dish with hot water and place this on the centre shelf. Two thirds fill the moulds, stand them in the water bath in the oven and bake for 25 to 30 minutes. Have heated plates at the ready if you want the creams to be at their lightest. Turn out the creams, coat each with sauce, to which you have added the shrimps at the last minute, and serve at once.

GRILLED SPRING CHICKEN WITH GRAPEFRUIT, GINGER, HONEY AND HERBS
Serves 4

2 × 1½-lb (750-g) spring chickens, cut in half

For the marinade:
4 tablespoons grape-seed oil
1 tablespoon grapefruit or lemon juice
1 teaspoon salt
1 teaspoon ground coriander, or ginger, or milled pepper
1 clove garlic, crushed
1 tablespoon flower honey

To garnish:
2 grapefruits, knife-segmented
1 tablespoon roughly chopped coriander leaves
1 tablespoon roughly chopped flat-leafed parsley
1 tablespoon snipped chives
2 pieces stem ginger, finely sliced

Mix all the ingredients for the marinade in a large bowl. Have your poulterer halve the chickens for you and chop away most of the backbone. Leave the halved chickens in the marinade for 2 hours or more, or overnight in the fridge.

Pre-heat the grill to a high heat. Lightly brush the grill pan with oil. Set the pan about 6 in (15 cm) from the heat and grill the chicken halves, best sides up first, for 3 to 4 minutes. Turn them and cook for a similar length of time on their insides. Lower the heat and continue to grill them, turning at 1-minute intervals, until they are brown, succulent and to your liking – depending on their size and on your particular grill, this will take 12 to 14 minutes overall. The honey will caramelise a little. This is intended. Brush with the marinade during grilling.

Half a minute or so before serving, arrange 3 or 4 grapefruit segments on top of each chicken half. Warm them through a little, and sprinkle with fresh herbs when arranged on the serving plates or dish, and with the sliced ginger pieces. This recipe is also ideal for a summer barbecue.

Note that the spring chickens (or poussins as we wrongly call them) should weigh a minimum of 1½ pounds (750 g) if they are to serve 2. Anything less than this and you should allow one whole bird per serving.

WARM DUCK SALAD
Serves 6
A salad which makes one duck go a long way – and you'll still have the legs left to grill for another light meal.

1 × 4 lb (1.75 kg) duckling, or 4 duck breast portions

For the marinade:

2 tablespoons soy sauce
1 tablespoon dry sherry
1 tablespoon olive oil
1 tablespoon orange juice
1 teaspoon salt
1 teaspoon ground coriander
1 teaspoon ground ginger
1 teaspoon ground mace
1 clove garlic, crushed

For each serving of salad:

2 good curly endive leaves
2 radiccio leaves
1 slice beefsteak tomato
2–3 slices cucumber
1 artichoke bottom
1 black olive, pitted

For the dressing:

¼ pint (150 ml) olive oil
2½ fl oz (65 ml) orange juice
1 tablespoon red wine vinegar
1 teaspoon honey
½ teaspoon salt
1 teaspoon mild French mustard
½ teaspoon milled black pepper
1 teaspoon finely grated orange rind

Have your poulterer remove the duck breasts and cut off the legs; keep them to use on another occasion, and keep the carcass to use for stock for beetroot soup. Make 5 or 6 shallow incisions into the fleshy side of the breasts, about ¼ in (5 mm) deep, running right across. Arrange, cut sides upmost, in a shallow dish. Mix all the ingredients for the marinade together well and pour over. Now turn the breasts cut sides down and leave for 12 hours, or overnight.

To make the salad, pre-heat 2 tablespoons of olive oil in a heavy-bottomed frying pan until smoking. Remove the breasts from the marinade and seal on both sides. Lower the heat a little and fry the breasts for 3 minutes on each side if you like the meat to be pink, a little longer if it is to be well done. Remove the breasts to a plate whilst you assemble the salad ingredients on separate plates or dishes and prepare the dressing by shaking all very thoroughly together in a screw-topped jar. Slice the still warm duck breasts in thin diagonal slivers. Arrange 3 or 4 slivers on top of each assembled salad. A few butter-fried bread croûtons can be added for extra crunch if liked. These too should be warm, or 'tiède', as the French say; the direct translation of 'tepid' sounds rather unappetising to the English ear!

STEAK AND KIDNEY PUDDING
Serves 6

The first of these suet crusts is herby and lemony, the second is a spicy crust. Either is good, neither is mundane.

For crust 1:

8 oz (225 g) self-raising flour
1 heaped tablespoon freshly chopped parsley
1 teaspoon grated lemon rind
Salt and freshly milled white or black pepper
3 oz (75 g) suet
2 oz (50 g) cold hard butter, grated
Juice ½ lemon and cold water to make up to 6 fl oz (175 ml) to mix

For crust 2:

8 oz (225) self-raising flour
1 level teaspoon baking powder
Salt and freshly milled white or black pepper
¼ teaspoon ground mace, nutmeg, rosemary or bay leaf
4 oz (100 g) suet
1 beaten egg made up to 6 fl oz (175 ml) with cold water

For the filling:

2 lb (1 kg) rump steak or best stewing steak, trimmed of all fat
8 oz (225 g) veal or ox kidney, skinned and trimmed
1 heaped tablespoon flour
Salt and freshly milled black pepper
1 oz (25 g) butter
2 tablespoons oil
1 large onion, finely sliced
8 oz (225 g) button mushrooms, sliced or quartered
½ pint (300 ml) red wine
½ pint (300 ml) beef stock (use stock cube NOT Oxo)
1 bay leaf
1½ dozen fresh oysters or mussels (optional)

Sieve the flour and baking powder into a bowl, add the herbs and lemon rind or spices, the salt and pepper. Lightly toss in the suet and/or grated butter, and stir loosely with a fork until evenly distributed. Make a well in the centre, add the egg and water mixture and gather into a softish paste with the fork. Turn on to a well-floured work surface and knead into a soft dough. Cut off a good quarter of the dough for the lid. Roll out the rest and line the basin.

Pre-heat the oven to 350°F (180°C), gas mark 4. To make the filling, cut the steak into 1-in (2.5-cm) cubes and slice the veal kidney (cube the ox kidney if used). Put the flour, salt and pepper into a large polythene bag and toss the steak and kidney in this until completely covered. Melt the butter and oil in a large heavy-bottomed frying pan until smoking. Fry the onions until golden brown, removing them with a draining spoon to an ovenproof casserole. Fry the floured meats in the oil until browned on all sides, adding more oil and butter if needed. This is best done in small batches, removing each batch with a draining spoon to the casserole. Add the mushrooms to the casserole, shake over any remaining flour from the bag and mix in. Cover with the wine and stock and add the bay leaf. Cook in the oven for 1½ hours.

Allow the mixture to cool. Add the oysters or mussels and their juices, if using. Fill the mixture into the lined basin to within ½ in (1 cm) of the brim, making sure you have the meat covered with gravy (the balance of the gravy is to be heated and served separately). Wet the edges of the pastry and fit the lid. Cover with buttered foil, make a pleat across the top to give room for the crust to rise and tie firmly with string (see diagram). Steam for 1½ hours.

If you employ the pan method of steaming the pudding let the water come at least two-thirds of the way up the sides of the basin and keep the water gently boiling, which is one stage further than simmering, topping up when necessary. If you use a steamer the water should boil at a steady rate and will need constant topping up.

STEAK, KIDNEY AND MUSHROOM PIES

Serves 6 to 8

Traditionally this English recipe is palish in colour, therefore the tendency to over-Frenchify it, as has been done in recent years by some cooks, is to be resisted. Long braising in red wine, even the inclusion of tomato purée, has become a habit in our efforts to improve things, but the natural flavour of the three ingredients ought not to be masked. I don't think they are in my revised recipe.

For the pastry shells:

12 oz (350 g) puff or rough puff pastry (commercial brands are excellent)

Steak, kidney and mushroom mixture:

2 lb (1 kg), to yield 1½ lb (750 g), rump or best braising steak, trimmed of all fat and cut into ½-in (1-cm) cubes
2 lambs' kidneys, skinned, trimmed and diced
2–3 extra lambs' kidneys for garnish (optional)
Oil for frying
1 oz (25 g) plain flour
1 teaspoon salt
Milled white pepper
4 oz (100 g) onion, very finely chopped
¾ pint (450 ml) beef stock or tinned consommé
6 oz (175 g) small white-cap mushrooms, quartered

Pre-heat the oven to 425°F (220°C), gas mark 7. Select 2 individual tins which will fit inside each other. This means they should taper somewhat and be approximately 4 in (10 cm) in diameter. Brush one inside and the other outside with melted butter. Roll out the pastry in a large oblong, 16 × 12 in (40 × 30 cm). Cut into 6 or 8 pieces. Line the tin with one of the pieces and trim off the edges. Prick all over with the tines of a fork. Fit the second tin inside, press well home. (You can use the old foil and bean technique for blind baking, but I think my way is easier and more successful.) Bake in the pre-heated oven for 15 to 20 minutes. Cool a little. Remove the top tin and return the shell to the oven if it is not completely crisp and golden-brown. Cool on a wire tray. Store the shells in an air-tight container.

Prepare the filling. Heat the oil until smoking. Brown the cubes of beef and kidney in small batches, removing each one when ready to a plate; sprinkle with the flour, stirring well in, and season.

Brown the onion in the residue fats. Return the meats to the pan, pour over the stock. Simmer, stirring from time to time, for 30 minutes or until tender. Add the mushrooms 10 minutes before the end of the cooking time. If you wish to top each serving with kidney, cut the kidneys in half, and fry quickly for 1 or 2 minutes on each side in a good knob of butter. Season well. Drain, and keep warm. Re-heat the shells at 275°F (140°C), gas mark 1 for a few minutes, fill with the mixture, and serve immediately.

SHEPHERD'S PIE FOR A PARTY
Serves 10 to 12

Shepherd's pie is to Britain what lasagne is to Italy. In my home it was always made with cold cooked minced beef – hindlift, a cut of beef rarely seen in the south. This was not so much left-over meat, as is often said, but more that extra meat was purchased with this further use in view.

Today, no matter how well our nostalgia serves us, I think it has to be acknowledged that shepherd's pie becomes a stunning dish when made with freshly minced raw meat. But, a word of caution: ensure that your butcher's mince is fat-free. If it's not, buy a piece of meat and mince it yourself after trimming it of all fat.

This recipe will serve ten to twelve good portions, and is ideal for a Sunday lunch after a drinks party, or any other occasion where a good tasty budget dish is called for.

3 tablespoons olive oil and/or butter for frying
1 lb (450 g) onions, finely chopped
3 lb (1.5 kg) best mince
1 × 5-oz (150-g) tube tomato purée
1 oz (25 g) flour
Salt and freshly milled black pepper
1½ pints (900 ml) stock, water or half red wine, half water
A pinch of mixed herbs

For the rich potato topping:
3 lb (1.5 kg) potato, steamed and well mashed
¼ pint (150 ml) double cream, heated with 2 oz (50 g) butter
Salt and pepper
1 level teaspoon grated nutmeg

Optional extras:
16 oz (175 g) Dutch cheese, grated
2 lb (1 kg) tomatoes, sliced
1 lb (450 g) mushrooms, sliced, seasoned and fried in 2 oz (50 g) butter

In a large heavy-bottomed pan, melt the oil and butter, and fry the onions until golden brown, stirring them around continually to ensure even colouring. Remove these to a dish while you fry the mince for a couple of minutes in batches. Return the onions to the pan and mix well in. Squeeze or spoon over all the purée, mixing well in. Sprinkle over the flour and season well. (Don't add the flour first or the purée will clog it and inhibit its thickening agency.) Stir in the water, stock or wine and the herbs.

If your pan is not of a type which will go into the oven, transfer the mixture to an ovenproof casserole which will be large enough to take the eventual creamy potato topping. Cover with a lid, and cook for 1 hour. Leave to cool in the oven. Skim off any excess fat.

If the mince is not to be used immediately, allow to cool completely before refrigerating; or cover with the potato topping, return the dish to the oven without its lid and bake at 400°F (200°C), gas mark 6 until hot, brown and bubbling.

If you want to make a more luxurious pie, then add the extra tomatoes and/or mushrooms before you put on the potato. Add the cheese, half before and half after the potato top has been added. In any of these cases the pie should be finished in the oven at 400°F (200°C), gas mark 6 until brown, and the temperature then reduced to 325°F (160°C), gas mark 3 for at least an extra half-hour to ensure the extra layer is hot and cooked.

To enrich the mince use wine or wine and water, plus a crushed clove of garlic and half a head of celery, finely sliced and fried at the same time as the onions.

I have been known to use instant mashed potato on occasions which, when reconstituted and whipped with cream, butter and nutmeg is unbelievably good.

PUDDINGS

In introducing what Michael always called 'puddings', I think it best to let him speak for himself from his *New English Cookery*, except for two thoughts. Little expresses his passion for bringing our past traditions to new life as much as his puddings; and the last line of the last recipe, the chocolate cake recipe, seems a good epitaph for a generous man and a great cook.

'I never advocate an over-indulgence of sweet puddings. I do, however, believe that a treat, once in a while, is good for us. If you decide to serve that treat at the end of an excellent meal, then it should be delicately prepared from the richest ingredients: thick

cream, unsalted butter with its unsurpassed flavour, bitter chocolate, aromatic liqueurs, farm eggs, flower-toned honey and fresh
fruits. You cannot go wrong if you remember that small is beautiful, where at one time large portions were the order of the day,
today even the pudding-loving British are happy with delicate
spoonfuls of luscious mousses and home-made ices to round off a
perfect meal.'

BURN'T CREAMS WITH GINGER AND RASPBERRIES
Serves 6

Burn't Cream must be included in any self-respecting book on
English cookery. This dish is best made as individual puddings in
small fireproof ramekins.

2 whole eggs and 2 egg yolks
½ pint (300 ml) single cream
1 oz (25 g) caster sugar
1 large piece stem ginger, finely chopped
1 teaspoon gelatine crystals dissolved in 1 tablespoon boiling water
4 oz (100 g) fresh or defrosted frozen raspberries
Icing sugar for glazed topping

To garnish:
1 extra piece stem ginger, sliced into 6
Whipped cream (optional)

Beat the whole eggs and egg yolks. Bring the cream, sugar and
chopped ginger to the boil, pour over the eggs, whisking all the
time. Mix in the small amount of melted gelatine. Divide the
raspberries evenly between 6 ramekins. Pour over the cream
mixture and leave to cool and set.

Pre-heat the grill to spanking hot. Dredge the top of the creams
with a good ⅛-in (3-mm) cushion of icing sugar. Wipe the edges
clean. Stand the ramekins in a tin of ice-cold water, slide this
under the grill and let the sugar melt to a good dark caramel colour. Cool, but do not refrigerate again as this will soften the crisp
layer of caramel. Decorate with a slice of stem ginger and/or a
blob of whipped cream.

CHOCOLATE PYE
Serves 8

My recipe for this elegant English confection has appeared many
times from my pen and kitchen, and is a favourite with diners both

at Walton's and The English House. Each time it's slightly different as I change my mind about things.

Originally, I used the 'crackling crust' of Hannah Glasse, the famous eighteenth-century cook, and filled this crisp biscuity shell with the chocolate-cream of the London Tavern's master-cook, John Farley. However, my TV viewers and readers had problems with the pastry as it tended to go 'wangy' when exposed to the moisture of the filling. Also there was a hazard, though be it a minor one, with the cream filling: it could – and for some did – curdle. So here is a Model Three: all safe, sound and easier to make, having lost nothing in the alterations I have made.

You should serve only a small slice: it's very rich and more-some.

For the pastry:
5 oz (150 g) butter, chilled
8 oz (225 g) plain flour
A pinch of salt
2 oz (50 g) sugar
1 egg yolk
3 tablespoons water

For the filling:
10 oz (275 g) dark chocolate
4 tablespoons sherry or rum
1 teaspoon gelatine crystals
2 tablespoons cold water
5 eggs, separated

For the garnish:
Whipped cream
Toasted walnuts or almonds
Chocolate flakes or squares

To make up the pastry, rub the cubed chilled butter into the flour and salt, working lightly with your fingertips, until crumbs are reached. Fork in the sugar. Beat the yolk and water together, add and knead lightly. Leave the pastry to relax in a fridge for 30 minutes before rolling.

In a round-bottomed bowl put the chocolate broken into bits, and sherry or rum made up to ¼ pint (150 ml) with cold water. (If sherry is used add 1 teaspoon vanilla essence.) Set the bowl over a pan of boiling water and allow the chocolate to melt and get quite hot. Stir in the gelatine softened in the 2 tablespoons of cold water, making sure it is totally dissolved in the chocolate mixture.

Remove the bowl from the heat and beat in the egg yolks one by one. Leave to cool but not set. Stiffly beat the whites and cut and fold these thoroughly into the chocolate mixture. Fill into the pastry case and put to set, but do not refrigerate (this will make the pastry go soggy). Decorate with a border of whipped cream, almonds or walnuts and chocolate squares or flakes.

For high days and holidays, you might be able to lay your hands on some gold or silvered almonds and some sugar rose petals or violets, which would make a truly opulent 'pye'.

REAL ENGLISH CUSTARD

Makes 1½ pints (900 ml)

This is the true custard for serving with steamed sponge puddings, fruit pies and pasties and is the all-essential sauce in trifle making.

1 pint (600 ml) milk (or half milk and half cream)
1 vanilla pod (or 1 teaspoon vanilla essence)
1½–2 oz (40–50 g) caster sugar
1 teaspoon cornflour
5 eggs

Bring the milk to the boil, together with the vanilla pod. Mix the sugar with the cornflour, add the eggs gradually and beat the mixture well until it is smooth. Remove the vanilla pod from the saucepan and pour the boiling milk on to the egg mixture, stirring all the time. Rinse out the pan, leaving a film of cold water in the bottom. Return the custard to the pan and stir it with a wooden spoon over a low heat until it is thick. Plunge the bottom of the pan into a basin of cold water to remove any residual heat which might curdle the custard. Leave to cool.

RICH RICE PUDDING

Serves 6 to 8

All the ingredients of a traditional eighteenth-century rice pudding are here brought back together again and enriched with cream. I like it best served cold, studded with candied or crystallised fruits. The subtle complement of an extra spoonful of unsweetened thick chilled cream is worth breaking the diet rules for.

1 pint (600 ml) milk
3 oz (75 g) Carolina (pudding) rice, washed
2 oz (50 g) caster sugar (or less)
¼ teaspoon grated nutmeg
1 teaspoon lemon zest
1 teaspoon pure vanilla essence (or pod)
2 oz (50 g) candied orange, finely diced, soaked overnight
in 2 tablespoons whisky
1 pint (600 ml) double or whipping cream
2 large egg yolks (if served hot)
1 teaspoon gelatine crystals dissolved in 2 tablespoons
cold water (if served cold)
Other candied or fresh fruits to garnish

Put the milk, rice, sugar, nutmeg, lemon zest and vanilla into a lidded double boiler. Boil until the rice is completely soft, about 45 minutes.

To serve hot, pre-heat the oven to 400°F (200°C), gas mark 6. Stir in the candied fruit, unwhipped cream and the 2 egg yolks. Transfer the pudding to a buttered 3- to 4-in (9.5- to 10-cm) deep dish. Stand this in a water bath and bake for 20 minutes until the traditional skin has formed.

To serve cold, stir the gelatine thoroughly into the cooked rice while it is still hot. Leave to cool. Gradually incorporate the candied fruit and the cream, which should be half-whipped to ribbon stage. Chill, covered with plastic film. Serve in a glass bowl garnished with extra candied fruits or flaked almonds. (The mixture will thicken somewhat as it chills.)

RICH PEAR TART
Serves 6 to 8

For the pâté frollé:
4 oz (100 g) plain white flour
1½ oz (45 g) ground almonds
1 egg yolk
3 oz (75 g) unsalted butter at room temperature
2 oz (50 g) caster sugar
¼ teaspoon vanilla essence

For the frangipane:
1 egg yolk
2 oz (50 g) caster sugar
2 tablespoons Kirsch
2 oz (50 g) ground almonds
3 large ripe pears

For the custard:
3 eggs
1 oz (25 g) caster sugar
½ pint (300 ml) single cream, chilled

To make the *pâte frollé*, pre-heat the oven to 425°F (220°C), gas mark 7. Sieve the flour into a bowl. Mix in the ground almonds with a fork. Turn on to a dry work surface. Make a well in the centre. Put in the egg yolk, soft butter, sugar and vanilla essence. 'Peck' at the mixture in the centre with the fingertips until it is well creamed, gradually incorporating some of the dry ingredients as you 'peck'. Now change to a palette knife and cut in the rest of the dry ingredients using a chopping movement with the edge of the blade. When a sandy texture is reached press the dough together, cover with wax paper or put into a floured plastic bag and refrigerate for at least 1 hour. Line an 8-in (20-cm) deepish flan ring and bake this blind for 10 minutes, then at 375°F (190°C), gas mark 5 for a further 10 minutes.

To make the frangipane cream the egg yolk and sugar. Add a tablespoon of Kirsch and beat in the ground almonds. Spread on the bottom of the pastry case. Peel, halve and core the pears and turn them in a basin with the remaining Kirsch (this prevents discoloration). Arrange them in a circle on top of the frangipane mixture, pointed ends to the centre.

To make the custard, well beat the eggs with the sugar, add the cold cream, pour over the pears and bake the tart at 450°F (180°C), gas mark 4 until the custard is set. This tart is better served hot or warm.

CHOCOLATE BRANDY CAKE
Makes an 8-in (20-cm) cake

3½ oz (65 g) chocolate (Terry's Bitter or Cadbury's Bournville or Peters)
1 tablespoon brandy
3 eggs, (size 2)
4½ oz (120 g) caster sugar
1 oz (25 g) cornflour
1½ oz (40 g) self-raising flour

Pre-heat the oven to 375°F (190°C), gas mark 5. Melt the chocolate with the brandy in a small bowl over a pan of simmering water. Meanwhile whisk the whole eggs and sugar until fluffy.

Dredge the two flours together and fold into the egg mixture. Pour in the melted chocolate folding well in with a metal slotted spoon. Pour the mixture into a buttered and papered (bottom only) 8-in (20-cm) sandwich tin. Bake in a pre-heated oven for 10 to 15 minutes. 'It's good. It's very rich . . . But my goodness it's more-ish!'

INDEX